Doris C.J. Chu

That Gentleman From China

IS Book

Copy right © by Doris C. J. Chu
This work is fully protected by copyright law. No deletions, substitutions, or alterations may be made by anyone for performance or otherwise without written consent of the author. No part of this work may be reproduced, translated, transmitted electronically or mechanically, or stored in any information retrieval system, or adapted for film, television or radio without the prior written consent form the author of this book.

CAUTION

The performing rights (including public reading) to this play belong exclusively to International Society. Amateur and professional theatre groups alike must acquire written permission and pay royalty to International Society before this work may be staged or read whether or not the performing group is for profit or not-profit, and whether or not admission is charged. Inquiries should be addressed to International Society via email to info@internationalsociety.us

Published by International Society Press
Web address: www.internationalsociety.us
Printed in the United State of America
All rights reserved

LCC 99-072494
ISBN 978-1-928730-04-0

Cast
Premiere production
1998

Narrator #1	Doug Holsey
Governor Bennett	
Mr. Henry Hentz	
Ralph	
James Strobridge	
P.C. Huntington	
Frank Pixley	
Mr. Cochran	
Senator Piper	
Joseph	
Narrator #2	John Herring
Governor Burnett	
Waldo	
Charles Crocker	
State Official	
William Ar-Showe	
Senator Sargent	
Narrator #3	Alexandra de Suze
Mary Little	
Narrator #4	Susan Hern
Josephine Hentz	
Mark Hopkins	
Narrator #5	Charles Hughes
Liang Ar Kan	
Governor McDougal	
Mr. Sullivan	
Governor Bigler	
Leland Stanford	
Butler in scene 15	
City Official	
Butler 2	
Senator Cooper	
Oong Ar Showe	Alex Chen
Understudy: for Narrator #3 and Mary	Holly Little
Louisa Hentz	Stacie Green

7

Cast
2000 Production

Actor/narrator #4   Ritza Elizabeth
Mrs. Josephine Hentz
Mark Hopkins

Actor/narrator # 5   Chris Wrenn
Governor John McDougal
White miner
Ralph
James Strobridge
San Francisco City Official
Mob leader
The butler in scene 15
Mr. Sullivan
Senator Cooper of Tennessee

Actor/narrator # 2   Tom Mazur
Joseph
Governor Peter Bernett
White miner
Waldo
Charles Crocker
P.C. Huntington
San Francisco City Official
Mob leader
William Oong
Senator Sargent of California
Gift bearer

Actor/narrator # 1   Dave Dobson
George the inn keeper
Judge Bennett
Mr. Henry Hentz
White miner
Governor Bigler
Leland Stanford
Frank Pixley
Mob leader
Mr. Cochran
Butler in scene 17
Senator Piper of California

Oong Ar-Showe   Joseph Salonga

Ar Kan   Rishard Chen

Mary   Lisa Remo

Louisa Hentz   Rochelle Fuentes Te

Playwright's Note

Some years ago when researching for *Chinese In Massachusetts, Their Experiences and Contributions* I came across some materials about a Chinese tea merchant in Boston in the 1850's. He immediately caught my attention and aroused my interest. His name was Oong Ar-Showe or Charles Ar-Showe. His last name was Oong. By piecing together some very scanty and not-easy-to-come-by data I learned that Oong had opened up a tea and coffee store on Union Street where a Citizen's Bank branch located at the end of the 20th century. He married an Irish girl, Louisa Hentz, of South Boston in 1852, had his first son, William in 1853. In April of that year he and his baby were both baptized. In 1860 he became a naturalized U. S. citizen. In 1866 he moved to Malden, then a gentry town. He had two daughters, Lizzie and Louisa, and another son who died at infancy. Oong's tea business was very flourishing. His investments in real estate and carriage service were highly profitable. He was a successful, wealthy and generous who funded the entire Centennial celebration in Malden including such events as float parade, firework displays and banquet.

His wife died in early 1878. Some Chinese from western Massachusetts came to the funeral. In the fall of the same year, he went back to China. Before he left a large farewell party was thrown in his honor. And in the following day, a group of gentlemen from Malden accompanied him to New York to see him off.

He was the first Chinese to marry a Caucasian American woman, to become a U.S. citizen, and to become a member of the Free Mason in Boston. At that time, when Chinese workers helping to build America's west in the Pacific coast were persecuted, Oong's social status was a blatant contrast. The historical data do not tell us why Oong suddenly went back to China. Nor do they give us any hint about Oong's inner self. I, however, suspect that he must have suffered a great deal of pain because he had violated the traditional value steadfastly upheld by the Chinese of that time: Loyalty, filial piety, integrity and righteousness.

He married not a native girl from his hometown but an American girl. he never brought her or their children back to meet his parents. In fact he never even visited them during all those years he was in Boston. These made him an unfilial son. He was naturalized. That might have required his relinquishing his Chinese citizenship. Thus he was not loyal to his country or his Emperor. He was proselytized to Christianity perhaps in order to fit in the American society. In that case he has compromised his integrity. I suspect that he did not willingly accept Christianity for obvious reasons:

An early attempt of Christianity to enter the Chinese soil was in the late16th century during the late Ming dynasty when Jesuit priest Matteo Ricci of Italy went to China. For a hundred years the Jesuits met strong cultural resistance and was unsuccessful in their religious mission. They, however, made remarkable contributions as cultural ambassadors. They enlightened Europe on China and informed China about Europe. In the 19th century when Christian missionary entered China their aggressive way of preaching, patronizing attitude, and irrational attack on the foundation of Chinese civilization, tradition and morality infuriated the educated gentry. The Christian missionary described China as "a country without a history and philosophy without substance" (Jeffrey Paul Chan, Frank Chin and others, ed. *The Big Aiieeeee*, New York, Penguin, n.d.) They portrayed the Chinese as being ignorant and cruel. The Confucian scholars, on the other hand, characterized Christianity as being ignorant, superstitious and seditious. The name of a Christian convert would be removed from the family register and he would be ostracized by the entire society. (Dun J. Li, The Ageless Chinese, a History, 2nd ed. New York, Scribners, 1971)

Although Oong was merely the son of a merchant which traditionally was not a respected class in China, he might very well be educated and shared the resentment of the scholar gentry class toward that foreign, aggressive religion.

The tragic experiences of the Chinese in the Pacific coast was a sharp contrast to Oong's privileged social status in Boston. Did he not feel guilty and useless because he could not do anything for his suffering compatriots?

If we think the treatment of immigrants and ethnic minorities in the United States is inequitable today, just imagine how it was over a hundred years ago! Oong must have felt he should not stay in this foreign land for too long. He was over fifty years old and his wife passed away. He must have felt It was time for him to return home, like a falling leaf returning to its roots. His children were all grown. The oldest son, William, was twenty-four. The youngest daughter, Lizzie, was eighteen. He did not have to worry about them any more as long as he left all his fortune to them. Take them to China with him? How would they adjust to the new environment with the language barrier, with their appearances of neither Chinese nor American? Why made them suffer the pain of being a stranger in a foreign land to be discriminated against?

Based on these thoughts I created the character of Oong Ar-Showe in *That Gentleman from China*.

I also suspected that Oong must not have been oblivious of the misery of the Chinese laborers in the West coast because the newspapers and magazines often printed cartoons and disdainful stories about them. A person with feelings and conscience, that he must have been one I suppose, would be deeply affected by those stories. In the play, I wove the glaring contrasts of Oong's story and those of the other Chinese in California into one. While enjoying prosperity and prestige, Oong could not help but feel sad. In the play he said: "Every time when I read about how much they were hated, despised, how much they were unwanted, I feel guilty."

In the end he resolutely left America. When questioned by his son, William, he sad: "Because China is my country. China is where my home used to be." He felt that despite his enormous wealth and social status in Boston he had not accomplished anything: "All my life what have I accomplished? Nothing. I made a lot of money. That's all. To the Chinese, merchants are not in a respected class. I gave much money to benefit the public. But I am not able to do a thing for my own compatriots."

Leaving his children behind also was a very difficult decision: "I am a Chinese living in America. I left my parents behind and never went home. To a Chinese this is most unfilial. I have neglected my duty as a son. Now, as a father, I am about to leave my children behind and go to China. To the American, this is most unfatherly. I have failed to be a good son and I am failing to be a good father." He said to his son: "China is not a place for you. You are a half American. You will not be accepted there."

There were only 54 Chinese workers in California in 1849 and 450 in 1850 the year Oong came to Boston. By 1860 there were 34,933 Chinese in the United States. In the beginning some of them were drawn by the glimmer of gold (Gold was discovered in 1848 at John Sutter's Sawmill, north of San Francisco.) But more of them were brought to the U.S. to meet the great need for manpower to develop the American West. They were warmly welcome in the beginning. Their hard work, frugality, and willingness to undertake any kind of work deeply impressed the employers. Many writers described them as industrious, persevering, resourceful and adaptable. They were paid much less than the white workers and worked from sunrise to sunset. Not only did they work in the mine, field, orchards, and fisheries industries, they also assembled pre-fabricated timber- and stone houses imported from China, and reclaimed the swamp-land. Most of all, they were the major work force building the transcontinental railroad.

The employers' favoring in hiring the Chinese provoked jealousy and antagonism among white workers. In 1852 the governor of California began to make anti-Chinese racist outburst which stirred up violence against the Chinese from one end of California to the other. In the following decades, the Chinese workers were blamed for economic downturns and the white workers' unemployment. Racism and paranoia among the white workers resulted in the massacres of Chinese laborers and ordinances against them. Contemptuous names such as "yellow peril" "coolie slaves" and "chinks" were labeled on the Chinese who were also classified as "inferior race... incapable of progress or intellectual development..." by white Americans. It was the latter's ignorance of other people's history and civilization that was responsible for their assuming a sense of superiority.

Before 1859 the Manchu imperial court (ruler of China then) forbade expatriation and imposed severe punishment for emigration from imperial China. Even after the law was relaxed, the government never encouraged its people to go abroad. China did not confer protection to its people in other countries unless they were sent there.

Although Oong Ar-Showe did not suffer the severe racial hostility himself, he must have been disheartened, nevertheless, by what he saw. He must have felt that no matter how much he did for the community, he would not be accepted by this country. As such, shortly after his wife died he left for China with a broken heart.

The intention of the play is not to blame or complain but rather to use history as a mirror for us to see the mistakes in the past so as to prevent them from repeating. Throughout human history many mistakes have been made everywhere and corrections have been made as well. The most constructive attitude, I believe, is forward looking, not constantly complaining about the past and demanding the current generation to pay for the mistakes of their forbearers. We have to agree that race issue in the American society today in comparison to that of the nineteenth century is like day and night. The Government has undeniably done everything, establishing policies and laws, and giving monetary compensation for example, to make up for past mistakes. In many cases racial discrimination is reverse to the disadvantage of the "white" Americans; preferential treatments are given to minorities. Many Caucasian Americans hold a apologetic feeling of guilt because their ancestors' behaviors in mistreating some groups of minorities. I think these are overdone and should be corrected. what we need is fairness and just.

--Doris Chu
Feb. 21, 2012

SCENE 1
The parlor of an inn, Boston, spring of 1850

Characters
Oong Ar-Showe, George the Innkeeper, Joseph, a friend of George's

>As the lights are up, **actors #4** and **#5** are on stage to make announcements.

Actor 4:
Scene 1, spring of 1850

Actor 5
In the parlor of an inn in Boston

>(Actors 4 & 5 exit stage right. George the hotel clerk is behind his counter. Joseph rushes in.)

Joseph (actor 2)
George, where is that foreign guest of yours?

George (actor 1)
Which foreign guest? We have a number of them here.

Joseph
I mean the one wearing fancy robes and a pigtail.

George
Oh, you mean that gentleman from China!
>(He puts his elbow on the counter.)

Joseph
China? Is that where he's from? How fascinating! Most people here have not seen a man from China before, except on the porcelain wares. This gentleman from China, what's he like? How long has he been here? Does he speak English?

George
Hardly, at first. But he hired a tutor. He's been here for three months. And he seems to be learning pretty fast.

Joseph
Can he understand me if I speak to him?

George
If you keep it simple.

Joseph
Hey, may I meet him?

George
Sure you may. Ah! Here he comes. Hello, Mr. Ar-Showe, any luck in finding a storefront?

Oong
Hello, Mr. George.
*(To **Joseph**)*
Hello, sir. Yes, a store, Union Street. Number 25.

Joseph
*(Extends his hand to **Oong**)*
Welcome, sir, welcome to Boston. Are you going to open a store here?

Oong
*(Shakes **Joseph**'s hand.)*
Yes, a tea store. The best tea. I am Oong Ar-Showe. You are?

Joseph
The name is Joseph Smith, sir.

Oong
Mr. Joseph.

(Lights off)

SCENE 2
California, 1850

Lights up. **Actors #4** and **#1** walk to down-stage to make announcements.

Actor 4

Scene 2

Actor 1

California, 1850

*(Both actors exit as **Ar-Kan** enters. **Ar-Kan**, dresses in Chinese peasant's loose pants and shirt, followed by a spotlight, enters stage left and crosses to down-stage center.)*

Kan

I am Ar-kan from Toishan, a small village of Canton province in China. I worked in a teashop in the city of Canton for a few years. The Americans said:
(Changes his voice and gestures to mimic the American merchants in China)
"America is a big country with lots of money and gold. We also have a lot of works to do. We need you to help us do those works."
(Changes to his own normal voice and mannerism.)
So we came. Our Emperor forbade us from going abroad. Violators would be decapitated.
(Gestures with his right hand swiftly slicing across his throat.)
We also did not like to leave our homes and families to toil in a foreign land. But wars, internal turmoil, natural disasters made life difficult for many people. The situation is the worst in my village. So many of us left the country to try our luck abroad. I borrowed money from friends and relatives so that I could pay my way to America. I promised to pay back the debt from my earnings. After the debt is paid we can save up some money. I can send that money home to my parents, as any filial son would do. We young men must sacrifice ourselves for our families. Since I am here, my younger brother has to stay home. One of us has to stay with the parents. We cannot leave our parents without care.
(Pause)
When I was small I learned farm-work from my father. Now, I work in the mine here in California

(Lights off)

SCENE 3,
Oong Ar-Showe Tea and Coffee Store,
Boston, fall of 1851

*(As the lights are up **actors #5** and **#1** are on stage to announce the characters in this scene. The characters enter as their names are announced. When some characters failed to come on stage a chaotic scene is resulted.)*

Actor 5

Scene 3, Oong Ar-Showe Tea and Coffee Store

Actor 1

Boston, Fall of 1851

Actor 5

Characters: Oong Ar-Showe,

*(**Oong** enters)*

Louisa Hentz,

*(**Louisa** enters.)*

Mary - Louisa's cousin

*(**Mary** enters.)*

Store clerk

(no one shows up.)

Stage Manager in the back stage

He is not here today.

(Some stir among the actors on stage)

Actor 5
(Continues to make his announcement.)

Customers.

Stage manager in the back stage
They are not here either.

(The director jumps up to the stage from the audience area.)

Director
What's going on? Where are those people? Why isn't the scene changed?

(**Stage Manager** emerges from backstage.)

Stage Manager
We have a problem. Half the cast is absent. We can't do the show.

(More stir among the five actors on stage.)

Director
What? Where are they?

Stage Manager
Some went to New York to audition for a Broadway show. Some got calls to do a TV commercial. You know, better opportunities, more pay, why not?

(The actors on stage react to the crisis in commotion.)

Director
(in ire)
Great. That's just great.
(begins to move the sets. to the others)
Can you give me a hand? Don't just stand there.

(Stage Manager strides over to help him.)
The show must go on.
(Shouts to backstage)
Hey guys, come out here.
(The other actors rush to the stage in confusion.)

Actors
Are we canceling the show?

Director
No, You know better than that. The show must go on. Get on it now.

Actors
How are we going to do it without them?

Director

Forget about the Store Clerk. Just play the Customers. Do multiple roles. After this scene I'll tell you what parts to play.

Actor # 2

Okay.

Actor # 1

Can we do it?!

Actor # 2

Sure we can. We have to. There is no choice.

Other actors

We know everyone's lines. Not a problem. Let's do it.

Director

Get on it now.
        (He claps his hands)
Hurry up!!

Everyone

All Right. All right.

*(The counter is moved to another location. A sign of "Oong Ar-Showe's Tea and Coffee Store" is put up. Director and Stage Manager exit stage left. **Oong** stands behind his counter speaking to two customers. **Louisa** and **Mary** look around the store. Other customers roam in and browse around.)*

Oong

Yes, I sell the best tea to Bostonians. Back home in Canton, we supplied large quantity of tea to the British and the Americans. I thought if the Americans liked our tea so much, why didn't I go there and give them the best and purest tea there was and show them the proper way to brew it and drink it.
        *(He notices **Louisa** and speaks to her)*
Madam, Do you often drink tea?

Louisa

Yes, I do. I like it. It's a little bitter. But I do like it. The sugar and milk take away the bitter taste.

Oong
(Smiles.)

Excuse me for saying so, but tea is best to be drunk as it is without adding sugar and milk. The initial slight bitterness will soon bring an aftertaste of mild sweetness. And it is clear and soothing.

Louisa

Mr. Ar-Showe, you said there was a proper way of making and drinking the tea. What is it?

Oong
(as if giving a lecture, accompanied by appropriate gestures)

You rinse the teacups and the teapot with warm water first. Put the tealeaves in the pot. Then pour boiling water in the pot and immediately pour this tea out and throw it away.

(He gestures throwing the tea away in a quick and jerky motion.)

This first brew is not the best. You fill the pot again with boiling water. Remember, the water must be boiling. Let the tea sit for one minute. Then quickly pour it into the cups in a circling motion so that the tea in all the cups have even flavor. No one is stronger or weaker than the other. You see, if you fill one cup at a time, the flavor in the first cup will be weaker than that in the last cup.

Mary

Good lord. We never thought of that.

Louisa

Because we put sugar and milk in it and cover the true flavor of the tea. Right, Mr. Ar-Showe?

Oong
(Smiles)

You are exactly right. Do you know how to drink it?

*(**Louisa** and **Mary** both giggle.)*

Mary

How **do** you drink it?

Oong

The cups are very, very small. You sip it a little at a time to savor the aroma and flavor. This is the art of drinking tea.

Louisa

Mr. Ar-Showe, you must show us how to make tea your way.

Oong

I will be most happy to do it.

(He takes out the tea set and begins to demonstrate tea brewing. Awe and admiration were written on everyone's face. He exaggerates the motions and interjects occasional remarks during the process.)

This water happens to be boiling. I rinse the pot .... Fill it with boiling water. ... And I throw it away.

(He throws the water to the back. The customer's backup to avoid being splashed.)

In China we measure the tea with our fingers. But now I am going to use this English teaspoon. One spoon. Two spoon, ... and a half... Now I fill the pot again. Then we wait. .... .And wait .... Now it's done. I fill the cups in circular motion.

(He hands the cups of tea to his customers.)

Please.

Mary

(Takes one sip. She doesn't like the bitterness but pretends to like the tea).

This is wonderful tea.

(Tries to hold back a grimace.)

Louisa

Um

(Makes a face over the bitter taste.)

It's really wonderful

(Other customers also praise the tea.)

Ar-Showe
*(to **Louisa**)*

Thank you madam.

(To others)

Thank you.

Louisa

Oh, we are so glad that you have this store here.

(She gets up and walks around a few steps.)

My father always comes here from South Boston just to buy tea and coffee.

Ar-Showe

Thank you madam. I don't think I have the honor of knowing who your father is. Perhaps I will know his name if you care to tell me.

Louisa

Mr. Henry Hentz. That's his name.

Ar-Showe

Oh, sure, Mr. Hentz. He is an old customer of mine. Since I opened the store over a year ago he has been my loyal customer. And we always chat about different things. My honor and pleasure to meet you, Miss Hentz.

(While he bows he extends his hand as a gesture of politeness.)

Louisa

(She puts her hand on his without thinking.)

My pleasure too, Mr. Ar-Showe

*(When their hands touch they are transfixed. They gaze at each other as if in a trance. **Mary** watches them from across the stage. She clears her throat to get their attention. **Louisa** awakes.)*

Louisa

This is my cousin Mary.

Mary

*(Extends her hand to **Oong**, smiles)*

Hello!

Ar-Showe

*(He Just quickly turns his head toward **Mary** and turns back to look at **Louisa**.)*

Hello.

*(**Mary** is apparently disappointed, embarrassed and insulted. She wants to get her cousin and leave.)*

Mary

Louisa,

*(**Louisa** does not hear her. **Mary** calls Louder)*

Louisa,

(louder yet)

Louisa!!

Louisa
(Suddenly wakes up from her dreamland.)
Huh?

Mary
(Walks to Louisa and takes her arm.)
We have to go now. ... Good day, Mr. Ar-Showe.

Oong
Oh, yes. Please wait.
*(He quickly crosses behind the counter, picks up a package and gives it to **Louisa**.)*
Miss Hentz, please take this tea as my humble gift.

*(As he hands **Louisa** the gift their hands touch. They are transfixed again. After a second, **Mary** pulls **Louisa** away.)*

Louisa
Thank you. Good-bye, Mr. Ar-Showe.

*(**Mary** drags **Louisa** to exit from stage right.)*

Ar-Showe
Good-bye Miss Hentz, Miss Mary. ... Come again.

(Lights off)

SCENE 4,
Welcoming the Chinese, San Francisco, 1850-52

(As the lights are up actors #1, #2, #4 and #5 are standing down stage narrating the historical background. Then they narrate the scene and introduce the characters.)

Actor 1

In 1850, the year when California became a state of the Union,

Actor 2

There were already 325 Chinese there, all of whom came in 1849 during the Gold Rush, like the other 100,000 men from the Atlantic coast of America and from Europe.

Actor 5

By the end of the year, 450 more Chinese came.

Actor 4

This vast state with its rich minerals, fine climate, and productive soil needed manpower to excavate and develop it.

Actor 1

The coming of the Chinese fulfilled some of that need.

Actor 2

As Alexander McLeod described in his book, *Pigtails and Gold Dust*: "In the first few years the Chinese were welcomed, praised and considered indispensable.

Actor 5

There was no race antipathy in those days. It was subordinated to industrial necessity and the Chinamen could find room and something more than toleration."

Actor 4

Characters:

Actor 1
(Announces the part he is playing. Then crosses to a chair and sits down.)

Judge Nathaniel Bennett

Actor 2
(Announces his part as an old man. Then he takes a chair.)

Governor Peter H. Burnett.

Actor 5
(Announces his own part. Then takes a chair.)

Governor John McDougal

*(A joyous, buoyant atmosphere filled with human voices and music created by sound effect. **Actor 1** strides up to downstage to speak. A spotlight follows him. **Actor 4** exits.)*

Bennett
On this occasion when we celebrate California becoming a new state of the union let me predict that America will soon become one of the wealthiest and most powerful nations on earth. California is rich in natural resources but we are short of manpower to develop them. Our Chinese friends are like our brothers. Although we were born and reared in different parts of the world under different political systems, and although we speak different languages we are now in the same country. We have the same dream and the same destiny.

*(The spotlight goes out. Another spotlight focuses on Governor **Peter H. Burnett** as he speaks to the legislators in the state house. This is in the year 1851.)*

Burnett
The Chinese come from one of the world's oldest civilizations. These people come here to help us develop our various enterprises and natural resources. They are our valuable assets and we should welcome them with all our heart.

*(The spotlight goes out. Another spotlight point at Governor **John McDougal** as he speaks to the legislators in the state house. This is in early 1852.)*

McDougal
Gentlemen, the Congress gave California those marshes and tidelands in 1850.

If we can develop them into useful farmland, their value will be tremendous. We should attract more Chinese immigrants to help us with this monumental task. The Chinese immigrants are one of the most worthy of our newly adopted citizens. California's climate is suitable to them because it is similar to that of South China.

(Lights out)

SCENE 5
Boston's Public Garden,
Summer of 1852

*(A Summer day filled with bright sunlight **Actors 1, 2, 4** and **5** are on stage to announce the scene and the characters.)*

Actor 1

And now scene 5

Actor 5

Summer of 1852,

Actor 2

Characters

Actor 4

Oong Ar-Showe

*(**Oong** enters from stage right and waits.)*

Actor 5

And Louisa .

*(**Louisa** emerges from stage right with a parasol. She and **Oong** strolls in the park. Music is up. Other park strollers tip their hats for Louisa as they gradually saunter off stage. Music fades out.)*

Louisa

Mr. Ar-Showe, I wish to let you know that these strolls in the park are very enjoyable to me.

Oong

Miss Hentz, these are the happiest moments of my days. I feel so lucky to be a friend of yours. I should thank Fate for bringing me to America to meet you.

Louisa

Perhaps this is God's will. Mr. Ar-Showe, do you believe in God?

Oong

I believe in a supreme power that is governing all the beings. It manifests itself in different ways, in different situations. We call it Heaven. If you ask whether I am a Christian, no, I am not.

Louisa

Are there any Christian in China?

Oong

Yes. There were American missionaries in China. They have proselytized quite a number of people. But the literati gentry class is hostile toward it.

Louisa
(astonished.)

Why is that?

Oong

Because the missionaries attacked the basic moral values and institutions of the Chinese society, which were cherished and safeguarded by the educated elites. Therefore, the converts are mostly the uneducated illiterates.

Louisa

Oh. Who are the educated elites, the literati-gentlemen? Are they nobility?

Oong

No, anyone, anyone at all has the right to get education. But there is no public school. If one has money, one can hire a tutor for his children and the children in the neighborhood.

*(**Louisa** closes her parasol.)*

Oong

If not, one has to find ways to join the rich man's private school. Or try to learn on his own. Then he takes a series of different levels of examinations -- local, provincial, then in the nation's capital, and finally, in the imperial palace. You must pass one level before you will be permitted to go to the next. Once you pass the second or higher levels of examinations, you are assured a post in the government. The highest social status is reserved for those government officials and scholars.

Louisa

Have you taken those examinations?

Oong

Only the first level. That was when I was 20. Two years later I left for America. I never had the chance to take the Provincial Examination.

Louisa

Would you have had a government position?

Oong

If I had passed the provincial examination I might have been appointed an office.

Louisa

Would you have liked to have that if you hadn't come here?

Oong

Yes, if I had stayed in China, I would have tried my best to earn a position in the government; be a respected scholar. But I chose to come to America because I was curious about this place. There were American merchants in Canton and my family did business with them.

Louisa

Mr. Ar-Showe, you are a fascinating man.

Oong

Dear Miss Hents, I think we should address each other by our first names now. Shouldn't we?

Louisa
*(Turns to **Oong**, bashfully)*

Yes.

Oong

Ar-Showe is my given name, actually. My surname is Oong.

Louisa

Oh, it's reversed.

Oong

Again, according to your custom.

Louisa

And everyone has been calling you Mr. Ar-Showe all this time.

Oong

I don't mind it as long as I don't have to reverse my name. We Chinese put our family names before given names because family comes first, self second. But in America you put your family names last. As much as I am willing to accept the American custom while I am here, I cannot reverse the order of my name. You see, we have a saying: "An upright person never changes his name." You may hear people say: "If I didn't tell you the truth I would reverse my name."

(Embarrassed by his own chattering. He begins to walk away.)

This is only to show that names cannot be reversed.

Louisa

So I should address you Ar-Showe instead of Mr. Ar-Showe from now on.

(She opens her parasol.)

Oong

Yes, please.

Louisa

Ar-Showe, Call me Louisa.

*(She shyly extends her hand to **Oong**, and turns her head away.)*

*(**Oong** takes Louisa's hand and delightfully shakes it.)*

Louisa

Oh, Mr. Ar-Showe, I mean, Ar-Showe, you are a fascinating man.

(Smiles. Closed her parasol and sits down on a bench.)

Oong

Thank you, my dear .... Louisa.

Louisa

What is Chinese courtship like? Is it arranged by the parents?

(Teasingly)

Have your parents chosen a girl for you?

Oong

*(Sits down next to **Louisa**.)*

In China, marriages are arranged by the parents. But not courtship. We do not have courtship.

Louisa

(stupefied)

No courtship? You mean young men and young girls just go on getting married?

Oong

(Smiles)

They are often engaged for a long time. Both families become very close. In fact, very often, the two families were already good friends, sometimes relatives. But the two youngsters are not allowed to go out together. They are not even allowed to see each other, usually.

Louisa

Then, how can they love each other -- total strangers?

Oong

They don't.

Louisa
(surprised)

They don't??

Oong

Not before the marriage.
(pause)
They feel obligated to marry the person of their parents' choice. Most often than not, they fall in love after marriage. They are not always total strangers either. Some know each other when they are little children because the families are friends or relatives. But they are not allowed to keep acquaintance when they grow up.

Louisa

What a strange custom!

Oong
(A little displeased.)

From the Western point of view.

(As he speaks he stands up and walks a few steps away

Louisa
(A little embarrassed)

I am sorry.

*(She stands up and walks towards **Oong**.)*

I know little about your culture.

Oong

East and West are a world apart. Our traditions and customs are diametrically different. But I am determined to learn about your culture. And I can learn it from you.

Louisa

And I can learn about you. I mean about China from you.
(Blushed, she sits down.)

Oong

I think our friendship will be more interesting than those of other people's
(He sits next to her.)

because we have so much to learn about each other and from each other. There are endless new things to discover.

Louisa

Yes, it sounds fascinating. You have not told me whether your parents have chosen a girl for you yet.

Oong

Yes, of course.

Louisa
(Apparently stunned and disappointed.)

Oh!!!!

Oong

It is a normal thing to do.

Louisa
(Upset, about to get up and leave.)

How interesting!!

Oong

Yes, she was a daughter of my mother's best friend. Our parents promised to tie the marriage knot between us since she was born.

Louisa

Since she was born!!?? That's ... so interesting
(Apparently vexed)

Have you met her?

Oong

Yes, In fact we were allowed to play together before I was ten years old. After that we never saw each other again.

Louisa
(She is trying to suppress her ire yet unable to escape from the pain inside.)

Do you remember her looks? Was she pretty?

Oong
(not noticing her changed mood)

Yes, she was a pretty little girl as I remember her.

Louisa
(exasperated)

Oh! How interesting!!!

Oong

Our parents were planning for the wedding. I was already twenty and she was eighteen. The right age to get married. And she...

Louisa
*(Peeved. Cannot bear to hear anymore she stands up in the middle of **Oong**'s speech. in a distant manner)*

It was a pleasure to have made your acquaintance, Mr. Ar-Showe. But we must say good-bye now.

(She turns away ready to leave.)

Oong
(Surprised at her displeasure, immediately gets up and follows her.)

Miss Hentz, wait. Have I said anything wrong?

Louisa

Said anything wrong? Do you expect me to keep acquaintance with an about-to-be-married man?

Oong

No, no, you got it all wrong.

Louisa

What did I get wrong? You are going to marry her, aren't you?

Oong

No, I can't.

Louisa

Why can't you?

Oong

Because she...she passed away.

Louisa
(Overwhelmed by this information she couldn't help feeling elated for herself but embarrassed for having that feeling. Her voice shows unrestrained joyousness.)

Oh, because she passed away!!! She passed away!! Oh, oh I am sorry. That's so sad.

(Pauses, hesitatingly)

Did your parents choose another girl for you afterwards?

Oong

No.

Louisa

Why not?
(Teasingly)
You were at the age to get married

Oong
(Flirtingly)
I guess they knew that I would come to America and meet you.
(He laughs.)

Louisa

Oh, Mr. Ar-Showe,
(Blushed. Gets up and crosses to downstage left.)
Be serious.

Oong
*(Follows **Louisa**.)*
I am serious.
(He grabs her right hand and kneels down.)
I believe our meeting was predestined. And Fate has prevented another girl from being chosen to be my wife.
(In essence this is his proposal.)

Louisa
(Joyous and shy, she puts her left hand on her chest and looks away.)
Oh!!!
*(Then she turns around to look at **Oong**, says the following line as a symbol of her acceptance of his proposal.)*
Mr. Ar-Showe I wish to let you know that these strolls in the park are very enjoyable to me.

Oong
(He confesses his true feelings for her.)
Miss Hentz, these are the happiest moments in my days. I feel so blessed to be a friend of yours. I don't know how to tell you...

Louisa
(She pours her heart out for him.)
Mr. Ar-Showe, you are such a wonderful gentleman. I have never met anyone like you. You are polite, gentle, kind, considerate ... and handsome ... and

strong ...

Oong

Miss Hentz, thank you for such kind words, which I do not deserve. I didn't dare to tell you, but ever since you came to my store eight months ago, I've longed to see you everyday. You've made my homesickness more bearable. I cannot help myself the way I feel about you. I hope you will excuse me for telling you this.

Louisa

No, no. I don't mind it at all. I feel the same way about you. I went to your store every chance I got. I told myself that I shouldn't... 'cause there is no future for us. I mean, I didn't even know what you would think. You would laugh, probably.

Oong

No, how could I? I didn't even dare dream that you would have fond feelings toward me! Especially, this distance between us--I am from China and you are an American.

Louisa

Exactly. That's why I say there is no future for us. If we fall in love that can only lead to a tragic ending.

Oong

But Miss Hentz, I have already fallen in love with you.

Louisa
*(Joyously, rushes toward **Oong**, almost bumps into him.)*
Oh, Mr. Ar-Showe, so have I. So have I. What do we do?

Oong

Maybe our love will not have a tragic ending. In fact, it will have a happy ending. I will see to it that it does.

Louisa

Are you sure, Mr. Ar-Showe? Are you sure?

Oong

Yes, I am quite sure. I believe in will power. When you are determined, nothing is invincible.

Louisa

Oh, I believe you. I believe you.

(Opens her parasol.)

Oong

I will send a message back home to let my parents know that I have decided to take you as my wife.

(Louisa sits down while Oong speaks.)

Louisa

(Overwhelmed with joy)

Oh!!

Oong

I will ask them to pardon me for not going home to marry a girl of their choice.

(He sits down)

And you must ask your parents to allow me to propose for your hand.

Louisa

(Suddenly reality hits her, worried)

Oh. I will try. I don't know what they will say. But I will try.

Oong

At least Mr. Hentz has known me for two years and he has no adverse opinions of me.

Louisa

No, he has often spoken fondly of you. But tying a marriage knot is another matter. I don't think there has been a single marriage between a Chinese and an American, ever.

Oong

Then we will make history. Isn't that wonderful?

Louisa

(Dreamingly)

Yes. We will make history. What about your parents? Will they oppose it? If we get married, you will stay here for as long as....

(Stands up and takes a few steps to downstage center.)

You will stay here. Will you? I am afraid I can't... I am not as adventurous as you are.

Oong

(Strides towards her)

Don't worry. I am already here. I will explain to my parents so that they will understand.

Louisa

Oh, Ar-Showe, I wish to let you know that these strolls in the park are very enjoyable to me.

Oong

Miss Hentz, these are the happiest moments in my days.

>(**Oong** looks around and sees no one around. He extends his hand to **Louisa**. She gives him her hand. **Oong** takes it with both his hand, then gently moves his hands upward from Louisa's hand to her shoulders. Then he pulls her toward himself and kisses her. At this moment the other actors (as stage hands) enter to set the stage for the following scene. They also seem to be strollers in the park (as characters in the play.) Their presence startled the couple. **Louisa** and **Oong** hurry off.)

(Light cue changes for the following scene without turning dark)

SCENE 6
Violence in the Mines, California, 1852

*(**Actors 1, 2** and **5** walk to the stage to announce the scene and characters)*

Actor 1
Scene 6, California, 1852

Actor 5
Since gold was discovered in California in 1848 people from all over the world went there to seek fortunes.

Actor 2
The Chinese did not come in large numbers at first. But even in 1849, when there were only a very small number of them working for mining companies, they were driven out by white miners.

Actor 1
In 1852, there were several thousand Chinese working in the mines. While the Governor openly praised them as one of the most worthy of the newly adopted citizens, the white miners were most antagonistic toward them.

Actor 5
In May riots broke out in the mines, demanding the Chinese miners to leave.

(All three announcers change into the characters of miners to play out the following short scene.)

Actor 2 as a white miner
Burn their tents. Kick them out!!

Actor 1 as a white miner
California belongs to the Americans, not the "demons with long tails."

(The scene of a riot is played out on the stage: Three actors represent a mob of miners. They shout at the audience. A sense of fury, frenzy, confusion and terror must be created through sound, lighting and violent actions.)

37

Actor 1 as a White miner
You dirty yellow pig. Get out of our mine.

Actor 2 as a white miner
America belongs to the Americans, not you damn Asiatics!

Actor 5 as a white miner
Burn their tents. Kick all of them out.

*(Lights remain unchanged. **Actor 1** gestures to end the violent scene. They then change back to be announcers to announce the following scene.)*

SCENE 7
Marriage Proposal

> *(In the Living Room of the Hentz's Home, South Boston, winter of 1852.* **Actors 5** *and* **2** *remain on stage to announce the scene.)*

Actor 5

Scene 7. In the living room of the Hentz's home in South Boston,

Actor 2

Winter of 1852.

Acto5

Characters: Louisa, Mary

Actor 2

Mr. Hentz, Mrs. Hentz, Oong Ar-showe, and Mr. Sullivan.

> *(**Actors 2** and **5** exit. **Louisa** and **Mary** enter. **Louisa** puts a vase on the table.)*

Mary

Louisa, Everyone is talking about you.

Louisa

What?

Mary

Louisa, its too risky.

Louisa

Huh??

Mary
(points to the chair)

Sit down.

(Both sit down)

Louisa, now, tell me. Do you really intend to marry that Chinaman?

Louisa

Yes.

Mary

What do you know about that Chinaman?

Louisa
(Look around)

Everything!!!

Mary
(Thinks of the worse, nervously she gets up, crosses toward stage right.)

Oh-----!! You didn't!! Louisa----!!!

(walks quickly back to her seat. Secretively)

Is he ...a good lover?

Louisa

Yes.

Mary

Will he be a good husband?

Louisa

I am sure.

Mary
(Looks around)

Can he love the same way our men do?

Louisa
(Looks around.)

He can love even better.

Mary

Oh----!! My goodness.

(Gets up from her chair. Crosses to downstage behind the chairs)

Louisa!! But he is a Chinaman.

Louisa

I know he is a Chinaman.

Mary

People will wonder why you don't marry one of our own. They will talk behind your back. He is different. And you don't really know this man.

Louisa

But I already know this man, Mary. People everywhere are basically the same.

(Stands up.)

Ar-Showe told me so. The difference is in their cultures and their looks. Once we cross the cultural barrier, we can think and act alike. Of course each person is different within a limit. Mary, He is a wonderful man. He is kind, gentle but strong, loving and considerate. I've never met anyone like him. I feel very comfortable and secure being with him. I am in love, deeply in love. He loves me so much, too. Mary, you don't know how happy I am; how lucky I am. You should be happy for me, too.

*(Kneels down by **Mary**.)*

Mary, my dear cousin, give me your blessing.

Mary
(concedes)

Well, I don't have anything else to say if you know what you are doing. Just be prepared for the worst. People may not leave you alone.

*(**Mr. Hentz** and **Mrs. Hentz** enter.)*

Louisa
(Crosses to her parents and kisses them.)

Hello mother. ... Father.

Mary
*(Follows Louisa. and kisses **Mrs. Hentz**.)*

Hello Aunt, Uncle.

(Returns to her seat.)

Mr. Hentz
*(Hands over a gift box to **Louisa**.)*

Daughter, this is from Mr. Sullivan. He said...

Mrs. Hentz
*(Cuts off **Mr. Hentz**)*

Oh, I think he is going to marry you finally. How lucky we are.

Louisa
(Throws the gift box on the floor.)

But I don't want to be married to Mr. Sullivan.

Mr. Hentz

Nonsense

(Picks up the gift.)

He's been courting you for four years.

Louisa

But I don't love him.

Mr. Hentz

Nonsense!

Mrs. Hentz

He is from a good family and a Harvard graduate. He will have a bright future.

Mr. Hentz

Your mother and I already gave him permission to make the marriage proposal.

Louisa

But I don't love him!!! Mother, sit down. Father, sit down. Listen to me.

*(**Mr.** and **Mrs. Hentz** are bewildered and not sure what to expect. They both sit down.)*

Louisa

I am in love with Mr. Ar-Showe. I am going to marry Mr. Ar-Showe.

*(**Mr.** and **Mrs. Hentz** were stunned. They get up from their seats. **Mary** gets on her feet too.)*

Mr. and Mrs. Hentz

What???

Louisa

Yes, I am going to marry Mr. Ar-Showe. He is a wonderful man. He is handsome, strong...

Mr. and Mrs. Hentz

You are not serious!!

Louisa

I am serious. I am in love Ar-Showe. I want to marry Ar-Showe.

Mrs. Hentz
(Faints and falls on the floor.)

Oh, God!

*(**Mr. Hentz** and **Mary** hurry to help her up and put her in her chair.)*

Mrs. Hentz
(faintly)

How could this happen?

Louisa
You have to accept him. He is going to be a member of the family.

Mrs. Hentz
Impossible!!

Mr. Hentz
We will not allow it!!

Mary
No!!

Mrs. Hentz
And he has not even asked for your hand yet.

Louisa
But he has.

Mr. Hentz
When? We have not accepted his proposal. We will not consider his proposal.

Louisa
Just the other day. I have **already** accepted his proposal.

Mrs. Hentz
Oh--!!!

*(She is fainting again. **Mary** fans her with a handkerchief.)*

What about Mr. Sullivan?

Louisa
What about Mr. Sullivan?

Mr. Hentz
Yes, What about Mr. Sullivan?

Louisa
I don't care about Mr. Sullivan. I love Mr. Ar-Showe. I am going to Mary Mr. Ar-Showe.

(Stumps her feet and dashes to downstage right.)

Mr. Hentz
(Stands up and crosses to Louisa, tries to pacify her.)

Dear daughter, what your mother and I concern about is your happiness. That's all.

Louisa
Then let me marry Mr. Ar-Showe. That will make me the happiest girl in the world. I love him!!!!

Mrs. Hentz
Dear, happiness is not a simple thing. There are many factors that make up happiness. Being in love is only one factor.

Mr. Hentz
We live within a society. What people do and think will affect us to be happy or unhappy. You understand what I mean, Louisa?

Louisa
Yes, I do, father. But I know nothing will affect my happiness as long as I am with Ar-Showe.

Mary
She sounds so sure.

Louisa
(chidingly)

I **am** sure. Mary, I am sure.

(A knock on the door outside.)

Louisa
That must be Ar-Showe.

*(See rushes to open the door. **Oong** enters followed by a carriage driver who is holding several gift boxes. **Oong** is wearing Western clothes complete with a top hat and white gloves. His queue has been cut. **Louisa** holds **Oong**'s hand with both of her hands.)*

Louisa
Ar-Showe, come on in.

(She turns around to speak to her parents.)

Mother, father, Ar-Showe is here.

Oong
(Still holding his hat in his head.)
How are you? Mr. Hentz, Mrs. Hentz, Miss Mary.

Mary
Hello.

Mrs. Hentz
(Still upset.)
Splendid!

Mr. Hentz
(Coldly)
Fine.

Oong
(Realizes that he is not welcome. He hesitates for a second. Then he composes himself.)
Oh, please accept these humble gifts.
*(Gestures the gift bearer to put the boxes on the table. The latter does so and clumsily knocks off Mr. **Sullivan**'s gift to the floor. **Oong** gestures him to pick it up.)*
Pick it up!!!
(The gift bearer clumsily looks around and cannot see it.)
Over there!!!

*(The gift bearer picks up the small box, looks at it. Then puts it on the table. He crosses to **Oong** and waits for his tip. **Oong** throws a coin at him. He catches the coin. Happily he bows to thank **Oong**. **Oong** waves to signal him to leave.)*

Oong
I thank you for letting me come today to beg you for your daughter's hand. I apologize that in the absence of my parents, I will have to be the one to come.

Mrs. Hentz
(Tries to regain her composure.)
It's all right. In America, marriage is not arranged by the parents anyway. You have every right to represent yourself.

Mary
Yes, You can represent yourself.

Oong
(Bows slightly)

Thank you.

Mr. Hentz
*(Gets up. Walks toward Louisa. Looks at her. Then walks to **Mary**. Looks at her peevishly.)*

Mary
(Timidly)

I don't know anything.

Mr. Hentz

Our concern is not about protocol. It is about the happiness of our daughter.
*(Dashes toward **Oong**)*
I have known you for two years. I think you are a fine young man. But whether you will be right for my daughter is another matter.

Oong

Sir, I will do everything to make your daughter happy. I know I am the right man for her.

Mrs. Hentz

But the racial difference, the cultural difference. We don't know anything about your country, your tradition and customs. Oh it's just too difficult. I am sorry.

Louisa
(Cuts in)

Mother, I love him!!!

Mrs Hnetz
(Continues)

I can see that you are an honest young man. Our daughter cannot be very wrong in her judgment. It's just ... marrying a Chinese ... that's never been done in Boston, in this Country.

Oong

Mrs. Hentz, I trust that you have many questions to ask me. You have to know more about me. Of course, I respect your concerns. It is risky to give away your daughter to a stranger, a foreigner. I would have many thoughts before I would marry off my daughter. Tell me how I can prove to you that I love your daughter very much, and that I am a trustworthy, sincere man. How can I convince you that China is a vast nation with a brilliant civilization and a very long history.

Louisa
(Cuts in)

They built the great wall.

Oong

I do not think that you would allow me to come to your house so that you can reject me.

Mr Hentz

Mr. Ar-showe, sit down please.

*(**Oong** looks at Louisa not sure what to do.)*

Louisa
*(Gestures **Oong** to sit.)*

He said please.

*(**Oong** crosses to take the 3rd chair. **Mr. Hentz** looks at him in wrath and pounds on the table. **Oong** stands up again.)*

Mr. Hentz
(Commandingly)

Sit down!!!!

*(**Oong** sits down again. Acerbated, Louisa dashes to downstage-left to face the audience, not looking at her parents at all.)*

Mr. Hentz
*(Darts to **Louisa**, accusatively)*

Louisa!

*(**Louisa** does not respond.)*

Mr. Hentz
(Louder)

Louisa!!

*(**Louisa** does not respond.)*

Mr. Hentz
(Yells)

Louisa!!!

*(**Louisa** turns to face the father for a second. Then turn away again irately.)*

Mr. Hentz
(Dashes to **Oong**)

Do you think you will still be allowed here if we do not take our daughter's happiness into consideration?

Mary

Everyone has to take into consideration what our friends and relatives will think and say.

Louisa

Mary, be quiet!!!

Mr. Hentz

You must promise us that you will never take our daughter to China.

Oong
*(Astounded by **Mr. Hentz** demand.)*

What???

Mrs. Hentz

You must promise us that you will never take our daughter to China!!!

Mary

You must promise.

Oong
(Stands up)

But Mr. and Mrs. Hentz...

*(**Mr. Hentz** points his index finger at the chair ordering **Oong** to sit down. **Oong** obeyed.)*

Oong

But Mr. and Mrs. Hentz, I must take my bride to China to meet my parents.

Mrs. Hentz

But we will not allow you to take our daughter to China at all.

Mr. Hentz

We will not allow you to take our daughter to China at all.

Oong

But this will be extremely unfilial on my part as a son. I cannot accept this demand.

Mary
(Gets up. Crosses to downstage)
You see It hasn't begun and already there are conflicts.

Louisa
(Irately)
Mary, will you be quiet.

*(**Mary** returns to her seat. **Louisa** turns to face **Mrs. Hentz**)*

Louisa
Mother, put yourself in the shoes of his parents. Think for them for a change.

Mrs. Hentz
Louisa, my dear, this is not any ordinary marriage. You know that I am not a heartless woman. It's just... I don't want you to go to that unknown place. God knows what will happen to you there.

Louisa
China is not an unknown place, mother. Nothing will happen to me there!

Oong
China is a great nation. Nothing will happen to her there!

Mary
But we can't be sure. We know nothing about China.

Louis
Mary!!

Mr. Hentz
Stop! Stop please.
(to Oong)
Do you wish to continue this conversation?

Oong
Of course I wish to...

Louisa
(Cuts in)
But father...

Mr. Hentz
*(Ignores **Louisa**. Speaks to **Oong**.)*
Then you must promise that you will never take our daughter to China.

Mrs. Hentz
You must promise that you will never take our daughter to China.

Mary
You must promise.

Oong:
(Defeated, he hesitates, struggles, finally resigned.)
I, ... I promise you.

(Dejectedly, he strides to downstage. To himself)
It's because I love her too much. Heaven forgive me. My dear parents, forgive your unfilial son.

Mr. Hentz
*(Comes up with another difficult question for **Oong**, like a bombshell.)*
Ar-Showe, Which church do you belong to?

Oong
I am not a Christian. I don't belong to any church.

Mrs. Hentz
(Appalled)
What? A heathen?

Louisa
Mother. He is not a heathen.

Mr. Hentz
What is your religion?

Oong
I ... I have no religion.

Louisa
(astounded by his answer)
Ar Showe!!!

Mr. & Mrs. Hentz and Mary
(Scream alarmingly.)

An atheist!!!

(Mrs. Hentz and Mary rushes over to pull Louisa away from Oong and push her toward stage left and hold on her tightly.. Louisa struggles and cannot free herself from their hold. Mary and Mrs. Hentz each presses one hand on the chests.)

Mrs. Hentz

Oh, God!!

Mary

It's sinful.

Mr. Hentz

How can you say you are from a nation of brilliant civilization? To be without religion is to be without morality. How could our daughter marry an immoral man?

Louisa
(Still trying to pull herself away from her mother and cousin)

Father, religion and morality are two separate things. Ar-Showe has explained it to me.

Mrs. Hentz

Of course he must say that. What else could he do? Admit that he has no morality?

(Louisa continues to try freeing herself from her mother and cousin but failed.)

Oong

Mrs. Hentz, we Chinese are governed by a set of very strict moral codes and ethical standards, which are above religion. We have total freedom to choose our religious relief or disbelief. But all have to abide to moral and ethical standards.

Mr. Hentz

I don't know what your Chinese moral standards are. We cannot allow an atheist in our midst.

Mrs. Hentz

Of course we cannot.

Mary

No, We cannot.

Louisa
(Tears herself away from her mother and cousin's hold.)

Ar-Showe told me that there were American missionaries in China. Christianity is an accepted religion there. Many Chinese were proselytized. He can be converted to a Christian too.

*(**Oong** is astonished by her remark. He quickly turns his head and gives Louisa a questioning glare.)*

Mr. Hentz

Then, you **will** be converted to Christianity.

Oong
(Again he is vanquished, hesitatingly he gives in.)

I ... I suspect that ... Christianity does not directly ... conflict with ... the Chinese Confucian thoughts. I ... I ... I will consider it.

Mrs. Hentz

This is an absolute requirement if you **are** to marry our daughter.

Mr. Hentz

If you wish to be accepted as a member of our American society it is imperative that you believe in our God. And there is no choice for you but to try to be accepted by the society if you are to marry an American girl.

Oong

I understand that. And I have every desire to become part of your society.

Mrs. Hentz

Then, join our church. Begin to study the Bible. In a year you will be baptized.

Oong
(Hopefully)
Does this mean that I am promised marriage to Louisa?

Mrs. Hentz

I don't know!!!

Louisa

Mother!!!

Mr. Hentz

I don't know!!

Louisa

Father!!!

Mr. and Mrs. Hentz
(Look at each other. Give in)

I suppose so.

Louisa
(Scoots to her parents and hugs them.)

Oh, thank you father. Thank you mother.

*(Then she dashes to **Oong**. They hold each other's hands.)*

Ar-Showe, you are right. Our love has a happy ending. Those strolls in the park are most enjoyable to me.

Oong

This is the happiest day in my life. Thank you Mr. and Mrs. Hentz.

(bows to them.)

I am most happy to be your son-in-law, and I should call you mother-in-law and father-in-law from now on.

Mr. Hentz
(Not ready to accept it)

Oh no, not so soon.

*(A knock on the door, Mary goes to open the door. **Sullivan** enters.)*

Oong

I give you my words; I will take the best care of Louisa, and love her forever with all my heart.

*(Kisses **Louisa**.)*

Sullivan
*(Sees **Oong** kissing Louisa)*

What is the meaning of this?

Mary: Mr.
(Makes a belated announcement)

Mr. Sullivan is here.

Mr. Hentz

It seems that my daughter and Mr. Ar-Showe are planning their marriage.

Sullivan

Miss Hentz, am I understanding correctly that you have chosen this worthless

Chinaman over me?

Louisa
(Steps up to Sullivan.)

You watch what you are saying!!

Oong
(Pulls Louisa back.)

Never mind him. Louisa.

(Crosses to face Sullivan)

One day, you will see this unscrupulous man bow to me.

Sullivan
(Turns to Oong, scornfully)

Me? Bow to you? Ha, ha! That's when the sun rises from the west and you become the emperor.

(He pokes his finger at Oong.)

Oong
(Throws Sullivan's arm away.)

We shall see. We shall see.

Sullivan
(Strides to upstage. Takes off his hat. Then he strides to the Hentzs. Bows lightly)

Mr. and Mrs. Hentz, Miss Flynn.

(Turns his head toward Louisa.)

Miss Hentz.

*(**Sullivan** crosses to stage right passing the table and stops. He turns around; makes a gesture as if about to speak. Then he sees his gift to Louisa lying on the table. He picks it up; laughs and exits.)*

Mary

This calls for a celebration.

*(**Mary** takes Louisa and **Oong**'s arms and exit together. Music cue.)*

(Mr. Hentz returns to being **Actor 1** and remains on stage. **Actors 2** and **5** enter for the next scene. Mr.s Hentz returns to being **Actor 4** and dances by herself on stage.)

Actor 1

What are you doing

Actor 4

I am working on my reaction to this happy occasion.

Actor 2

Ritza (actor 4's own name) what are you doing?

Actor 4

I told you. I am working on my reaction to this happy occasion.

Actor 5

But what about the next scene?

Actor 4

Next scene? You mean the wedding scene?

Actors 1, 2, 5
(In unison)

California!!!

Actor 4

California? That's your business. Now I have to go change my costume.

*(**Actor 4** exits.)*

(Lights out)

SCENE 8
Governor Bigler's scheme, California, 1853

*(**Actors 1, 2, 5** are on stage introducing the scene and characters.)*

Actor 2
John Bigler was the Governor of California for two terms during 1852-1855.

Actor 5
On April 23, 1853 he gave a speech in which he denigrated the Chinese workers as coolie-slaves and strongly advocated the exclusion of the Chinese.

Actor 2
He was the first politician to use anti-Chinese sentiment as a weapon to win ballots from the working class.

Actor 1
He was also the first one to label Chinese workmen as slaves.

Actor 2
It was later proved by the Federal and California State governments-- through careful investigations -- that the Chinese young men were free people in China and that they came to the United States on their free will.

Actor 1
The scene takes place in the Governor's mansion.

Actor 1
(Announces the role he is playing)

Governor Bigler

(He takes a seat in center stage.)

Actor 2
(Announces his role)

His campaign advisor, Waldo

*(He takes his position standing by the side of **Governor Bigler**.)*

Actor 5
(Announces his role)

And Ralph, a labor representative

*(He crosses over to stand behind **Bigler**.)*

Waldo

Governor, our white miners do not want the Chinese to work in the mines. The Chinese have no right there. We have to stop them. They are a great threat to us.

Bigler

Why?

Ralph

Because they take the jobs away from us. The employers preferred them to the white men.

Bigler

Why is that?

Waldo

Because they work harder and accept less pay. They also are ready to take any job that the white workers don't want.

Ralph

Our white workers cannot compete with the Chinese. But California belongs to white Americans. Governor, you have to do something. You cannot allow the Chinese to take away what is ours. Unless we kick them out we can never have peace. Governor, as an elected official you should listen to your voters. There are many more working class men than company owners. And each man has one vote.

Waldo

Ralph, the Governor is fully aware of that.
(instigatingly)
Governor, we cannot win next year if we do not have the miners' votes.

Bigler
(Awakened)

Of course I will listen to what the majority wants. We must think of a good strategy, a good reason for excluding the Chinese. The difficulty is that the Chinese are peaceful and law biding. What reason do I have to attack them?

Ralph

There are plenty of reasons. The Chinese have irritated the white men in our state. They have caused us misfortunes. They are stupid and uncivilized. Aren't these good enough reasons?

Bigler

Uncivilized? That is hardly convincing. Many of us know that China is a highly civilized nation. Didn't they build the Great Wall?

Ralph

But these are peasants. They are not the civilized Chinese.

(Changes his tone of voice)

Their wooden, inexpressive faces make me so angry; it makes me want to slap them.

Bigler

Let's think of some good reasons to get ride of them. We need issues.

(Lost in deep thought.)

Ralph

We need concrete action. We should enact an ordinance that will restrict the Chinese from employment. Levy extra taxes on them. That might stop more of them from coming.

Bigler

But our Foreign Miners tax already targets the Chinese. This tax brings the largest single item of income to our state treasury. The white immigrants are exempt from it because then can naturalize to become citizens. The Chinese are the only foreigners who are not eligible for naturalization. What I can do is to increase the amount of Foreign Miners tax every year as long as I am the governor.

Waldo

You will give an important speech on April 23rd. That will be a good time to announce your position on Chinese immigration.

(He broods for a second.)

Got it. Convince the public that the Chinese are slaves. Our society cannot tolerate slavery. That should disturb them enough. Whether the Chinese are slaves or not is beyond the point. We just have to convince the public. And the fact that the Chinese in California are all bachelors gives us a good basis to say that their wives are being held hostage in China as a guarantee that these coolie slaves fulfill their contract faithfully. We will convince the public that this servile class of people is harmful to our democracy and dangerous to the welfare of the state. We cannot allow these people in our midst.

Bigler

But our people know that the Chinese are not slaves.

Waldo

That will change. We must make them change their mind. Slaves are not allowed to testify in court. Our law prohibits the Negroes and Indians from that. This can easily be applied to the Chinese. Without access to our judicial system, or legal protection, their existence will be so hard that they might not want to stay here any longer.

Ralph

What legal protection? They never had any to begin with. Those disgusting rats don't deserve it.

Waldo

Tell the public that America belongs to white Americans. We will do everything to ensure that. The Chinese must be denied the right to citizenship because of their inferiority.

Bigler

The Federal government may call these ideas unconstitutional.

Waldo

But when an issue is crucial to the welfare of a state, the state government has the power to make the decision. The Federal Government has no jurisdiction over the state government in such a situation.

Bigler
*(Thinks for a second, to **Waldo**)*

Well then, Waldo, prepare a speech for me for April 23rd. Emphasize these points: Prohibit the Chinese from naturalization; allow no Chinese from giving evidence in court; and we cannot permit that servile class of useless, dishonest and inferior people in the state of California.

Waldo

To substantiate the last point, we will give concrete evidence. There are 500,000 criminals in China. They are all trying to come to America as slaves. They will endanger the American public with pestilence as foul as leprosy and the plague. This should sufficiently scare the public.

Ralph
(Laughs)

That is good.

Bigler

And stress these points: We must use heavy taxation to force those already here to leave the state; we must petition the Congress to issue a ban on Chinese immigration.

Ralph and Waldo
(Joyously)

Governor, the state of California thanks you.

(Lights out)

SCENE 9
Christening of Oong Ar-Showe, Boston. April, 1853

(As the light come up, **Actors 1, 2, 4** *are on stage announcing the scene and characters in the scene.)*

Actor 2

Scene 9

(Exits after making the announcement)

Actor 1

Christening of Oong Ar-Showe

Actor 4

Boston, April 1853

Actor 1

Characters:--

*(**Actor 7** enters and announces his role in the scene.)*

Actor 7

Oong Ar-Showe

*(**Actor 8** Enters and announces his role in the scene.)*

Actor 8

Louisa

Actor 1
(Announces his role in the scene.)

Mr. Hentz

Actor 4
(Announces her role in the scene.)

Mrs. Hentz

Actor 3
(Announces her role in the scene.)

Mary.

*(**Actor 2** Enters with a baby)*

Actor 2

Baby William, only 2 months old.
> *(He hands the baby over to **Mrs. Hentz**.)*

Mrs. Hentz
(talks to the baby in her arms.)
God bless you, my dear grandson. Are you having a good time? Umm?

Mr. Hentz
Two new Christians in our family.

Louisa
Ar-Showe, when are you going to tell your parents?

Mary
(Happily, she turns a full circle.)
His name is Charles now.

Mrs. Hentz
Yes, I like that name. "Charles" is so much easier to say. I'll bet your friends will like it better, too.

Oong
(Not at all interested)
I am not used to it yet.

Mary
It will take some getting used to. Charles, are you going to tell your parents about your new name, too?

Oong
There is a Chinese saying: "A righteous man does not change his name." That means if a man has done nothing wrong he need not hide himself behind a fake name.

Mary
Come now, no more of those Chinese sayings.

Mr. Hentz
Why? You don't like them? I think it's kind of fun. Charles always tells us about these little peculiar things.

Louisa
(a little annoyed)
Father, when you are away from home I think it's natural that you think a lot

about things back there.

Mrs. Hentz
I guess that is the only way to keep himself kind of still connected with China. Right, Charles?

Mary
I suppose one needs to feel connected with one's native land.
*(to **Oong**, changes the subject)*
Charles, is Christening an important event in China?

Oong
I don't know. I didn't know anyone personally who had become a Christian.

Mrs. Hentz
Which would be a bigger event? The birth of your son or your wedding anniversary?

Mary
(Excitedly)
Wow, one in February, one in March. Plus your Christening in April. Three big events in a row. This is a great year for you two.

Louisa
Ar-Showe told me, in China, a wedding anniversary is nothing. On the other hand, the birth of the first son is a big occasion. When the baby is one month old, there would be a big banquet. Lots of gifts from friends and relatives. It's almost as important as a wedding.

Mr. Hentz
That's why your parents sent the gold locket and gold bracelets to the baby. And those funny looking cute little shoes.

Louisa
It is customary for the babies to get those gifts. Those shoes with tigers' heads are meant to expel evil spirits and to protect the baby's health.

Mrs. Hentz
But that's superstition. That's so un-Christian like.

Louisa
Mother, that's just a folk believe. Ar-Showe said they would dye eggs red and gave them to all the guests at the baby's first month celebration banquet.

Mary
Dye eggs red? We do that on Easter.

Oong
(Disinterested, even a little fretted)
Yes, perhaps in both cases egg symbolizes life. There is no superstition there.

Mrs. Hentz:
I think baptism is a beginning of a new life. Charles' parents may want to dye eggs for Charles and the baby.

Mr. Hentz
Anyway, today is an important day for Charles. He is a Christian now. And he's got an American name. Who knows, some day he may become a full-fledged American. Son, I am proud of you. You are doing all right. A thriving business, a good red-blooded American wife, a beautiful baby, what more can a Chinaman want? You are doing all right.

Oong
(To himself, dejectedly, softly)
Yes, but I wish my parents could see the baby.
(Decidedly, in a firm and louder voice.)
I will take my son to China.

Mrs. Hentz
But going to China is out of the question.

Mr. Hentz
You promised not to ...

Oong
This is their first grandson. How could the grandparents not see their grandson?

(Oong takes the baby from Mrs. Hentz and walks toward stage right. The Baby cries. Mrs. Hentz weeps. Louisa looks at her parents, then crosses to Oong. She takes over the crying baby; cradles him. The baby is still crying. She crosses to her mother, hands the baby to her mother. Oong not expecting Louisa's action, turned away in wrath.)

Mrs. Hentz
(Embarrassed by the tense atmosphere, she makes an excuse to leave the room)
Let me go see if everything is ready for the party. The guests are about to come any minute.
(Mrs Hentz and Mr. Hentz exit stage left.)

Louisa
(Sympathetically, helplessly, she tries to soften the atmosphere.)
Maybe we can send them a picture.

Oong
(fretted)
A picture?

Louisa
(Feeling uneasy for having made an inappropriate suggestion, awkwardly she uses the same excuse as her mother's to leave the room)
I... I'll go see if the guests have arrived.

*(**Louisa** exits stage left.)*

Mary
*(Quickly crosses to **Oong**. Holds his hand.)*
Oh. Charles, this is your happiest day. Don't let anything spoil it. Cheer up. I am so sorry that Louisa has said the wrong thing.

*(**Oong** is dispirited, his head lowered.)*

Mary
*(Holds **Oong**'s head with her hands and kisses him.)*
You know how I feel about you. Charles, don't be sad.

Oong
*(Unexpected of **Mary**'s action, gently removes **Mary**'s hands from his head. sincerely)*
Mary, thank you for your kindness. I'll never forget that. But you know I love Louisa.

(Lights off and on again)

SCENE 10
Central Pacific Railroad Company, 1865

*(**Actors 1, 2, 4, 5**, are on stage making announcements)*

Actor 4
Central Pacific Railroad Company, 1865

Actor 1
Before the first transcontinental railroad was built, a journey from the Missouri River to San Francisco would take six months by horse and covered wagon.

*(**Actor 2** plays out the treacherous journey.)*

Actor 4
The need to link California and the eastern states was urgent.

Actor 5
In 1862 Congress voted funds to build the 2,500 mile long railroad from Omaha in the East to Sacramento in the West. The Central Pacific Railroad Company took on the job of building the railroad from Sacramento eastward and the Union Pacific Railroad Company would build from Omaha westward.

Actor 2
On January 8, 1863 the ground was broken in Sacramento.

*(**Actor 2** enacts a scene of ground breaking.)*

Actor 1
In two years, only 50 miles of track were laid because few people wanted the job. The Company could not get more than 600 workers and many would take off after payday only to come back for the next check.

Actor 5
As a last resort, Charles Crocker, one of the four owners of the Company in charge of construction, insisted on hiring Chinese workers.

Actor 2

The scene takes place in an office of the Central Pacific Railroad Company.

Actor 4
Characters:

Actor 5
(Assumes his role in this scene)
Leland Stanford, President of Central Pacific Railroad Company

Actor 1
(Assumes his role n this scene.)
James Strobridge, the Superintendent

Actor 2
(Assumes his role in this scene.)
Charles Crocker, one of the Big Four, in charge of railroad construction.

(Actor 4 exits stage right)

Crocker
We really must resolve this problem. Since we broke ground on January 8 of last year, almost two years have gone by. Only 50 miles of track have been laid! With this speed how many years will it take us to build our half of the 2,500 miles. Congress only gave us 14 years to complete the job. We have 12 left.

Strobridge
I know it. I am just as vexed as you are. It is so hard to recruit workers. We advertised for 5,000 and we never got more than 600. After payday they clear out to get drunk and get into trouble, only to come back for the next paycheck. These hoodlums are unstable and unreliable. They only want to make quick money, not to do the hard work.

Stanford
Is there anything we can do? Will more pay help?

Strobridge
We are paying them $35 a month plus food that costs about $1 a day.

Crocker
That's not bad pay. Paying any more will eat into our profit. James, I think we should give the Chinese a shot.

Strobridge
No, I will not boss Chinese. I don't think they can build a railroad. They are small and skinny. I doubt they have the strength, the durability and skill.

Crocker
They built levees and roads in San Francisco. And they have helped build a railroad in California. Why don't we give them a try.

Strobridge

It's too much trouble. The Chinese eat different food. And their way of living is different. It will make my job too difficult.

Crocker

It will not. We don't need to provide for them. They cook their own meals. Right there we save thirty dollars per day on each worker. They don't complain about anything. There is no bother.

Strobridge

I don't trust that they can build a railroad culvert either. That masonry work will be too hard for them.

Crocker

Didn't they build the Great Wall, the biggest piece of masonry in the world?
*(To **Stanford**)*
Leland, what do you say?

Stanford
*(Does not agree with **Crocker**.)*

Charles, You must still remember my position on the Chinese issue when I was the governor. I rigorously advocated their exclusion from our state. I proposed to the state legislature that they enact laws to prohibit Chinese immigration. And I condemned the Chinese as an inferior class of people so depraved that their influence would be detrimental to our superior race. This is only two years later. I would be embarrassed to contradict myself like that.

Crocker

Well, Leland, that was two years ago. You are not the governor now. You are the President of the Central Pacific Railroad Company. You have a different set of concerns now. And having the railroad built on schedule is the top priority among them. Wasting time is wasting money. We have no more time to waste.

Stanford
*(Still not convinced, to **Strobridge**)*

James, what do you think?

Crocker

We should just hire ....

Stanford
*(Cuts short **Crocker**'s remark)*

I am talking to James, not you.

Crocker
*(Prompts **Strobridge**.)*

Yea ... just give 'em a try.

Strobridge
Give 'em a try.

Crocker
Let's hire 50 of them.

Strobridge
Lets hire 50 of them.

Crocker
If we don't like them, let them go.

Strobridge
If we don't like them, let them go.

Crocker
If they are good, hire more. How's that?

Strobridge
If they are good, hire more.

Crocker
How's that?

Strobridge
How's that?

Stanford
(Convinced)
That sounds wonderful. Well, James. Let's build the railroad.
*(He shakes **Strobridge**'s hand and ignores **Crocker**.)*

(lights off)

SCENE 11
Naturalization of Oong Ar-Showe, 1860

*(When the lights come up **actors 1 and 5** are on stage to announce the scene and characters.)*

Actor 5

Scene 11

Actor 1

Naturalization of Oong Ar-Showe

Actor 5

1860

Actor 1

In the dressing room of the Oong's Malden residence.

*(The narrators exit. Enter **Louisa**, **Oong** and **Mary**.)*

Mary
(Waves an American flag in her right hand)
Oh, Charles. Congratulations. You are now an American citizen. A full-fledged American citizen! The first Chinese to be naturalized. A wealthy American citizen, too.
*(**Mary** holds **Oong**'s hands and turns a circle with him.)*

Oong
(Proud and confident)
Yes, a wealthy American citizen. It's great to be wealthy.

Mary
*(Lets go of **Oong**'s hands and runs over to **Louisa**.)*
Louisa, what jewelry are you going to wear this evening? You will stand out again among those rich ladies. The diamond necklace is splendid. That will be good for any color of the gown. The ruby and the emerald are gorgeous. I guess you have to decide which gown you are going to wear.

Louisa
(Apathetically)
How about the dark green satin and my emerald ear rings and necklace?

Mary

I think that will be fabulous. How about wearing your jade bracelets too? The pair that your mother-in-law sent you? Oh, that green is almost as brilliant as the emerald.

Oong
*(Smiles and strides over and puts his arm around **Louisa**'s waist.)*

I don't think jade and emerald will go together. Louisa seldom mixes different types of jewelry.

Mary

That's because Louisa has so many sets to choose from. Other women would be lucky to have any.

Louisa
*(Smiles proudly and looks at **Oong** a little sarcastically because she is not happy about **Mary**'s affection for **Oong**.)*

Because other women are not as fortunate as I am to have married such a wonderful husband.

*(She gives **Oong** a kiss on the cheek.)*

You see, my husband is not only a very successful businessman, he is my good advisor too. He has such fine taste. The things that he bought me are all extraordinary.

Oong

Because I have an extraordinary wife. She deserves the best.

Louisa
(Shows off to her cousin)

Mary, I have told you that he is a wonderful man.

(Repeats the same praise she always uses.)

He is kind, gentle, strong, loving and considerate. And I love him so much.

*(To **Oong**)*

Dear, you are truly the one that is extraordinary.

Mary

Look at you love-birds. After eight years of marriage you are still on your honeymoon! Well, I will leave you two alone. I'm going to join the guests in the ballroom now. You two hurry along.

*(**Mary** exits stage left.)*

Oong

This citizenship business is real magic. I do feel differently now. I feel like an

American as much as everyone else. I feel that I belong here. This is my home. For the first time, I really feel this is my home.

Louisa

Oh, Ar-Showe, I am so glad. You know, I've always felt so guilty that because of me you can't go back to China. But if you want me to go with you, for a visit, I mean, I will go.

Oong

Don't feel that way, my dear. I made a promise. We have a saying in China, "Once a gentleman gives his words, even four stallions can not chase them back." Ha ha, I haven't cited any Chinese saying for a while, have I?

Louisa

No, you have not. And I miss that. I like learning about China through your stories and sayings.

Oong

I have just about used up all there is to tell you about China. Now I am an American. A full-fledged American!! I am comfortable and happy here.
(Looks around)
I would not have all of this if I were in China. For one, as a merchant I would not have enjoyed the respect as I have here. In America, money speaks.

Louisa

Isn't it true in China too?

Oong

Well, money does not mean power in China. Power and prestige belong to the scholar-gentleman class.

Louisa

And that was why, when William was born you said you wanted him to be a scholar when he grew up ... to be among the gentry class.

Oong

(Strides to the dresser and looks at himself in the mirror and straightens out his shirt and tie. In the absence of an actual mirror, this can be played by having him walk downstage and face the audience.)
I don't think that way now. He is an American living in this society. I want what's best for him here, not what would be the best if he were in China ...

Louisa

Ar-Showe, when you speak at the Masonic Lodge next month, what are you going to talk about?

Oong
Oh, I have not thought about a topic yet.

Louisa
Will there be other new members giving speeches?

Oong
No. I think they only asked me.

Louisa
They have so much respect for you, as we all know. After your nomination everyone voted you in.

Oong
I plan to donate money to the Lodge. I think I should begin to give more back to the society that made my success possible. Dear, this is where you will be my advisor. You choose the worthy charities.

Louisa
That's easy. There have been a number of them trying to get me on their committees.
(Smiles)
.... meaning to get your money.

Oong
You should join them. Find out what they do and whether that's what you like.

Louisa:
Thank you, Dear. It will give me something fun to do.

Oong
If it will require time from you. We should hire a nanny for Lizzie. Cynthia is too busy just doing household chores. You are happy with the new cook, are you not?

Louisa
He is good. I have tried to teach him to make the two Chinese dishes you taught me. But he hasn't gotten it yet.

Oong
I don't mind not having Chinese dishes. I am used to American and European food now.

Louisa
Ar-Showe, you are so wonderfully easy-going.

(Lights off)

SCENE 12
Completion of the First Transcontinental Railroad, 1869

(When the lights come up actors 2, 4 and 5 are on stage to narrate the scene and introduce characters.)

Actor 5

Scene 12

Actor 2

Completion of the first Transcontinental Railroad, 1869

Actor 1

From February of 1865 to May of 1869, a period of three years and three months, with ninety percent Chinese in its work force, the Central Pacific Railroad Company completed the western part of the first transcontinental railway.

Actor 2

The western part with its treacherous terrain and inclement weather was much harder to build than the eastern part.

Actor 5

They had to conquer the solid granite of the Sierra Nevada. And when winter came the ground was frozen solid and there were sixty-foot snowdrifts.

Actor 4

It only took them four years and three months to reach Promontory, Utah where the two lines, one from the east and one from the west, were linked.

Actor 2

A big ceremony was held on May 10, 1869. Leland Stanford driving a golden spike into the last tie of the tracks with a silver hammer marked the climax of the ceremony.

Actor 4

Characters:--

Actor 1
(Assumes his role)

Leland Stanford, President of the Company

Actor 5
(Assumes his role)

C. P. Huntington, Vice President of the Company

Actor 4
(Assumes her male role)
Mark Hopkinton, Treasurer of the Company

Actor 2
(Assumes his role)
Charles Crocker, a part owner of the Company

Actor 4
(As the actor/narrator)
The scene takes place in an office in the Company's headquarters.

Huntington
That was a great ceremony. How much exactly have we made?

Hopkinton
We netted at least $63 million and our company's stock is worth around $100 million. And the four of us own most of the shares. Plus the 9 million acres of land granted to us by the Federal Government.

Stanford
It's amazing that we completed the line in six years, less than half the time we were given.

Crocker
In fact the first two years didn't count. Remember, we only got 50 miles of track laid in those two years. This wouldn't have been possible had we not employed the Chinese.

Hopkinton
Just in the 4 years we saved 5 million dollars because we paid the Chinese less and didn't have to provide them with meals.

Huntington
The important thing is that they were available. Where would we have gotten 15,000 workers, if it were not for the Chinese?

Crocker
Even if we were lucky, and we paid a lot more money to entice white workers and got 15,000 plus men, the job would not have been done until much later because they would not have had the incredibly high endurance for hardship and total dedication to their work, as the Chinese did.

Stanford
I am certainly impressed by their dexterity, ingenuity and extraordinary speed. 10 miles and 1,800 feet of track laid in a day -- that's a record I don't think anyone could break.

Crocker
They were paid 28 dollars a month instead of $35. And they took care of their own lodging and meals.

Huntington
They worked fourteen, fifteen hours a day. I wonder how they got time to cook.

Crocker
Oh, They didn't cook their own meals. They had a peculiar system. Each gang of workers hired a cook to cook their meals. Grocery suppliers follow them along the way. Each gang also had a headman who managed everyone's wages and expenses.

Hopkinton
That worked fine for them.

Crocker
That is very true. But 1,400 of them died while building the railroad.

Stanford
Is that really true?

Everyone
(In unison)
Yes, 1,400...

(lights off)

SCENE 13
Respected Resident of Malden, 1866

*(**Louisa** sits in a chair embroidering. **Oong** sit by a table reading. This part of the stage is dark. Only downstage where the announcers are is lit. **Actors 1, 2** and **4** are standing downstage)*

Actor 1

Scene 13

Actor 4

Respected resident of Malden

Actor 2

1866

Actor 1

in the sitting room of Oong's new home in Malden

*(**Actors 1, 2** and **4** exit stage right. **Louisa** and **Oong**'s area is now lit.)*

Louisa
Ar-Showe, our annual charitable gifts are getting too big. New charities keep being added to the list. Both Wilson Academies are asking for contributions. Since William is attending Wilson Andover we must give to that school. Should we keep the other Wilson on the list too?

Oong
You decide what to do, dear. Give to your favorite charities or give to the government.

Louisa
We are paying the highest tax of all residents in Malden. I don't mean that's not fair. But just our property tax alone is enormous. Then there are taxes on your investments and businesses.

Oong
Of course the more money one makes the higher tax one will pay. I think we should give more too. But set a limit if you like.

Louisa
People say you are more generous than many other very wealthy people. The society circle always speaks so fondly of you. And everyone wants to have you attend his party.

Oong
There are too many parties. We are always either giving parties or being invited to parties.

Louisa
But that's how the society circle is. Before I married you, my parents and I did not even dream of belonging to the high society.

Oong
Do you really enjoy it, Louisa?

Louisa
Yes, I do.
(Puts down her embroidery, reflecting on her happy and affluent life. She smiles and gets up to cross to downstage)
To be in a class that everyone respects and looks up to; to have more money than you need; and to help people with money.
*(She turns to face **Oong** who is now standing next to her.)*
I think it is wonderful.

Oong
(Smiles, takes her arm,)
As long as you enjoy it I am happy.
(They exist stage left.)

(All the actors quickly and quietly move to the back of the auditorium behind the audience, ready to play the mob in the following scene.)

(Lights off)

Scene 14
Anti-Chinese riots of 1876

*(As the lights come back on **actors 1, 2, 4,** and **5** are on stage to narrate the scene)*

Actor 1

Anti-Chinese agitation reached another climax in 1876-77. Bloody riots erupted throughout the state of California.

Actor 5

Chinese were beaten or killed, their houses burned, their belongings looted, Chinatowns were ransacked.

Actor 2

The employers who hired Chinese workers were threatened. Some were murdered.

Actor 4

The Chinese crowded into San Francisco's Chinatown, not daring to venture into other parts of the city. They lived in terror and misery.

Actor 1

Two events are represented in this scene. One is a public meeting on April 5, 1876, outside of San Francisco's United Meeting House.

Actor 5

A crowd of 25,000 peopled gathered at the plaza. The meeting was called by the Mayor of San Francisco and chaired by California's Governor, William Irwin.

Actor 2

The other is one of those riots at Sandlot in front of the City Hall.

Actor 4

Characters: --

Actor 1
(Announces his role)

Frank Pixley, a San Francisco City official and a leader of the anti-Chinese movement

Actor 2
(Announces his role)

State Official

(Actor 2 goes down the stage to the audience area.)

Actor 5
(Announces his role)

City Official

(Actor 5 also goes down to the audience area.)

Pixley
(Crosses to downstage center)

California should be a state for white men only. No other race should be allowed here. We must exclude the Chinese. Why? Because they are pernicious to our state. We must expel them immediately.

(He holds up a small pamphlet.)

Mr. Samuel Gomper, the President of the American Federation of Labor, said in this pamphlet

(reading form the pamphlet)

"Racial differences between American Whites and Asiatics would never be overcome. The superior whites had to exclude the inferior Asiatics, by law, or if necessary by force of arms." We agree with him. The Chinamen eat rice, fish and vegetables and we eat beef, bread and potatoes. We are radically incompatible even in the most basic things. We must petition President Grant and the Congress to enact a law that will exclude the wily yellow peril from ever coming to our country.

(He steps down stage to play the mob. The crowd reacts in fury. The atmosphere is tumultuous. Violence is about to erupt any moment. The actors representing the mob shout in response to the speaker on the stage.)

City Official
(Crosses to downstage center)

The Chinese are dangerous and deleterious to our society. And there are too many of them. California and the other western states are becoming a Chinese colony. They even have their own government and court inside their merchants' guild, the Six Companies. Can we allow the existence of a nation within our nation? Can we allow California to become China's colony?

(Actor 5/City-Official steps down the stage to play the mob. The crowd is now in fury and frenzy. Frantic emotion permeates the air. Loud noises override the speaker's voice)

State Official
(Goes to the platform to continue with his speech.)

We must have laws and ordinances to exclude them. Existing law that bans their children from our schools is not enough. They do not deserve to be in our schools anyway. Our white superior children cannot mix with and be influenced by those dirty yellow children. Not allowing the Chinese to testify in our court is perfectly called for. As Chief Justice Hugh Murray declared

(He reads from a sheet of paper.)

"The Chinese were a people whose mendacity is proverbial, a race of people whom nature has marked as inferior.... incapable of progress or intellectual development beyond a certain point, as their history has shown, differing in language, opinion, color and physical conformation; between whom and ourselves there has been placed an impassable difference."

(He lifts his eyes from the paper to look at his audience.)

The good judge of our Supreme Court has said it so well. But this law is not enough to restrict them. We need more. Let's sign this petition, my fellow countrymen.

(He waves a document in his hand.)

We will take this to Washington to the President and the Congress.

*(The stage darkens. Instantly stage right is illuminated. An anti-Chinese rally scene in this illuminated area is under way. This one is led not by the politicians but rather by disgruntled workmen. The location is Sandlot, a vacant lot in front of the San Francisco City Hall where many anti-Chinese rallies were staged in the years of 1876-77. Thousands of people filled Sandlot and the nearby streets, listening to the speech of **Denis Kearney**.)*

Kearney (played by Actor 1)

My fellow citizens. Who caused this depression that has lasted for years? The Chinamen, right?

Crowds

*(Roars in response to **Kearney**'s questions.)*

YES! The chinks.

Kearney

Who robbed us of our jobs?

Crowds:
(hysterically)

The chinks!
The yellow peril!
The dirty Chinamen!

Another speaker (played by Actor 2)

We must unite ourselves for the cause. We want the companies to stop employing Chinamen. We must boycott any goods manufactured by Chinamen. And we demand that all providers stop providing the businesses that employ any Chinaman. Those who employ Chinamen should be exterminated. The ships of the Pacific Mail Ship Company must be destroyed. **The Chinese must go! The Chinese must go!!** But look.

(He points to a helpless Chinese who happens to pass by.)

There is a Chinaman. What should we do about him?

(He jumps off the stage.)

Crowd
(in fury)

Beat him up!
Kill him!
Hang him!

(Violence erupts. The Chinese man is being kicked, slapped and punched. Someone pulls his queue and he falls down.)

(The playwright suggests that the mob scene may be suggested through the use of sound effects or played out from the audience area.)

Another mob leader (played by Actor 5)

(Jumps up to the stage. He shakes his fist and grinds his teeth.)

We must wring his neck so tightly his heart stops pumping and his blood stops flowing. Then we will throw him in the ocean.

(He sees another Chinese.)

There, another one. Get him! Hang him with his own queue!

*(**Actor 5** jumps down from the stage. **A third mob leader,** Played by **Actor 2,** jumps up to the stage from the audience area.)*

Third mob leader
We can only hang all the chinks, four hundred million of them, with their own queues because there is no rope long enough to hang them all.

> *(As the Chinese man is being beaten and strangled by the mob, a white passer-by shouts at the top of his lung in rage.)*

Passer-by
(played by Actor 4)
> *(Shouts from the audience area)*

Stop it! Let him go! You bloody murderers. What has he done to you? Why do you hate the Chinese so much?

> *(This **passer-by/Actor 4** tries to push the others aside to rescue the victim. But he too is knocked down immediately by the mob. The crowd becomes more obstreperous.)*

Kearney
Let's raid Chinatown. Get them out of their holes. Everyone of them!! Don't let a single Chinaman escape.

Crowds
Yes, let's ransack Chinatown.
Let's burn it down.
Let's go. Go!

> *(All the actors run up the stage to play a violent, destructive scene. The sound of a gun shot or explosion followed by sudden silence. Everyone freezes.)*

Actor 4
> *(Resumes his role as an actor/narrator. To the audience)*

The author and the director suggest that you use all your available faculties to imagine the violent scenes of these events. But now, we all need to take a break. There will be a 10-minute intermission.

INTERMISSION

SCENE 15
The year 1870
Oong's sadness, William's fight

(Actors 1, 2, 4, 5 introduce the characters)

Actor 1

Year 1870

Actor 2

In the drawing room of Oong's home in Malden

Actor 4

Characters:--Louisa, Oong Ar-Showe

Actor 1
(Announces the role he plays.)
Mr. Cochran, the Headmaster of Wilson Academy.

Actor 2
(Announces the role he plays.)

William, now 16 years old.

Actor 5

The butler

(Actors 1, 2, 4, 5 exit. Oong and Louisa enter.)

Oong
(Sadly)
Louisa, you know what day is today? It's the 100th day after the death of our son. It's also the mourning day of my mother's passing seven months ago. To lose a mother and a son in the same year! That is too cruel. Heaven was jealous of me because my life was too perfect.

Louisa
(just as sad, tries to console)

I know, I know.

Oong

Lately I have a strange feeling. I feel something is going to happen. Something is going to change. I... I have dreams some nights. I dreamt that I was in a small boat, drifting in a vast ocean ... alone.
(Dejected)
I didn't know where I was drifting to. I had nothing. It was so empty. I ... I am afraid... I am going to lose all that I have.

Louisa

Ar-Showe, don't scare me.

Oong

It's true. Nothing is permanent.

Louisa

But our love and happiness...

Oong

I lost my mother; I lost my father, and my son. I'm afraid I will lose everything.

Louisa

Ar-Showe, don't say that. I also lost my parents and our son. But thank god we still have William, Lizzie, and little Louisa. And we have each other.

William

(Dashes in from stage left. Deeply disturbed, he throws his bag on the floor.)

I am not going back to the school.

Oong and Louisa

William. What happened?

William

I had a fight in school.

Louisa

Oh, God. Why did you have a fight?

Oong

You never fought with anyone before.
(Very upset)
We taught you to be a polite gentleman. A gentleman does not fight. He reasons.

William
(Excitedly)
This boy insulted me. He was picking a fight with me.

Louisa
(Pacifying)
All right, all right. Tell us all about it.)

William

This boy, Scott, ... He said: "Why is a coolie slave's son allowed in our school?'

Louisa

Good Lord!!

William

And he called me "chink" and said, "Where is your pigtail? Why aren't you wearing the black pajamas like all the other yellow perils do?"

Louisa

Who is this boy? I can't believe there are such a scurrilous youngster at the Wilson Academy. We've never seen such....

William
(Cutting short Louisa's words)

Everyone else in our school isn't like that. I've never heard such malicious words before. This boy is new. They just moved here from California.

Oong
(Comes to a sudden realization.)

No wonder! There has been trouble for the Chinese working class people in California.

Louisa

Do you know what his father does?

William

He is an editor of the WASP.

Louisa

You mean the magazine?

William

Yes. The magazine. He threw pages torn off from that magazine and some newspapers at me and told me to look at the cartoons.
(Cries)

That filthy rascal.
(in a huff)

Father, why didn't you tell me about these things? Why are your people being hated so much? What have they done? Why are they slaves? Father, did you come here as a slave?

Louisa
(Irately)

William, watch how you speak to your father.

Oong
(To Louisa)

That's all right, dear.

(To William, sternly)

The working class Chinese in California or elsewhere on the West Coast are not slaves. They are uneducated, poor peasants, **but not slaves**. You remember that! They have not done anything wrong. They are hated by the American working class because the employers prefer them to others. As for me, my dear son, do you think a slave would be given the chance to rise to where I am.

William

Why are they being called all sorts of ugly names and being despised then?

Oong

I don't have a good answer to that.

William
(in despair)

What should I do, father. What am I? Am I an American any more? Or am I a Chinese? I have never thought about it.

Louisa

William. I think you are both. Isn't "both" better than "one"?

William
(Despondently)

No! Come to think of it, I am "**none**".
(Cries)

I'm neither American nor Chinese. I look differently from the other boys. And I certainly look very differently from the Chinese depicted in the cartons.
(Emotionally)

Father, why did you come here? Why did you marry mother?

*(**Louisa** weeps, covering her face with her hands)*

Oong
*(Rushes to **Louisa**'s side to embrace her. To **William**)*

I came here to see America, to meet your mother and to bring you to this world.

William

But there is no place in the world for me.

Oong

Nonsense, someday I will take you to China. Take all of you to China.

William

I don't want to go to China. I don't want to be here either.

(**Butler,** *Played by Actor 5, enters from stage left.*)

Butler

Mr. Cochran of Wilson Academy is here.

(**Cochran,** played by Actor 1, *Enters from stage left*)

Cochran
(very humbly)

Hello, Mr. and Mrs. Ar-Showe.

Oong, Louisa
(Not looking at him)

Hello.

Cochran

Hello William.

William

Hello, Mr. Cochran.

Cochran
(Anxiety in his eyes)

Mr. and Mrs. Ar-Showe, I came here to apologize to you about what happened this afternoon. I deeply regret that such a thing should happen at the Wilson Academy. I was not present, of course. I was informed afterwards and I came as soon as possible. I hope you would excuse the ignorance of a young boy. By the way, we already disciplined that boy, Scott Jones. He is being suspended for a week.

William
(To himself)

Serves him right.

(**Oong** glares at **William**.)

Cochran
(Searchingly)

I hope this is a just punishment. It is so unfortunate. We teach our students to be polite and gentleman like. But...

Louisa

We know. William has told us. This Scott is new. He just moved here from

California.

Cochran

Yes. I deeply regret this, nevertheless.

Oong

Although I do think William should not have fought with the boy, but the boy's despiteful attitude and language are inexcusable. If he is not made to fully understand and admit that he is wrong, that youngster will grow up to be an awful bigot, the kind of man that will only do harm to the society.
(Sternly)
Do you understand me?

Cochran

You are perfectly right, Mr. Ar-Showe. What do you think we should do?

Louisa

I think the boy should apologize to William. In fact, I think his parents should apologize too. They have not taught their son proper behavior.

Oong
(Agreeing with Louisa)
Exactly, we Chinese have a proverb. "To rear a son without teaching him right from wrong is the fault of the father." If the parents do not bring up the boy properly, the school has the grave responsibility of enlightening them.

Cochran

Yes, Mr. Ar-Showe. Yes.

(Lights out)

SCENE 16
North Adams, Massachusetts

*(This scene is presented in the form of narration by **actors #4** and **#5**. They stand at the front of downstate. The stage is dark only spot lights shine on the two actors.)*

Actor 4
In 1870, the year after the completion of the first transcontinental railroad, C.T. Sampson, owner of the largest shoe factory based in North Adams, Massachusetts, went to California and hired 75 young Chinese workers to break a strike of the union men, The Knights of St. Crispin.

Actor 5
They signed a three-year contract with Sampson.

Actor 4
When they arrived at North Adams depot on June 13, 1870 a large crowd of strikers and by-standers waited, shouting and throwing stones at them.

Actor 5
The police escorted them to their dormitory.

Actor 4
Within a few days of their arrival, some of them were capable of turning out complete shoes far better than those made by the average workers the factory had hired before. Both the speed and quality of production of the Chinese workers were higher than those of the Crispins.

Actor 5
Reports indicated that the Chinese workers saved Sampson $40,000 in production costs a year, a very large sum at that time. The profit increased while the prices of shoes went down.

Actor 4
50 more Chinese were hired the following year.

Actor 5
This contributed to strong and widespread anti-Chinese sentiments. A number of eastern newspaper editors began to call for exclusion measures against the Chinese.

Actor 4
Nevertheless the Chinese workers at North Adams were not treated too badly.

Actor 5
Sampson liked them.

Actor 4
The townspeople were friendly.

Actor 5
Some women even offered to teach them English.

Actor 4
The churches invited them to join.

Actor 5
Their diligence and good behavior won them a great deal of praise.

Actor 4
Even the Crispins relaxed their hostility and commented: "No one hundred and fifty men of any nationality could live together as these Chinamen are doing without having trouble among themselves, from drinking, etc."

Actor 5
The climate in Massachusetts was apparently much more affable than that of California. The Chinese workers felt at home and happy.

(**Actor 4** turns a circle to signify a change of scene from 16 to 17.)

(End of scene 16, Lights stay on)

SCENE 17
Meeting of Ar-Kan and Oong Ar-Showe, 1870

*(A continuation from scene 16 without lighting change. The turning in a circle by **Actor 4** suggests the change of the scene. **Actor 5** exits. **Actor 1** enters to join **Actor 4** to introduce the scene.)*

Actor 4
Meeting of Ar-Kan and Oong Ar-Showe

Actor 1
You remember Ar Kan. He was from Taishan and came to the States in 1850 to work in the minds. He was hired by C.T. Sampson in 1870 to work in the shoe factory in North Adams.

*(While **Actor 1** is speaking, **Actor 2** enters form stage right. He crosses to stage left from behind the narrators.)*

Actor 4
(Looks to her right and announces)
Oong Ar Showe

*(**Oong** enters and crosses to center stage by the table.)*

Actor 1
(Looks to his left and introduces.)
William

*(**William** enters.)*

Actor 4
In the living room of Oong's home in Malden.

Actor 1
Wait a minute, are we forgetting Louisa?

*(**Louisa** enters.)*

Actor 1
Here she is. That's right. And I will play Oong Ar-Showe's butler John.

*(**Actor 1** and **William** exit stage left. **Actor 4** exit stage*

right. **Actor 1** enters again carrying a big money case.)

Oong
John, bring it over here.

John
Yes, Sir.

(Puts the money case near the table. Then he exists stage left)

Louisa
What is it?

Oong
Oh, it's the money from three stores.

Louisa
Shall I put it in the save?

(About to pick up the case.)

Oong
No, no!! It's much, much too heavy. I will tell John to put it in the bank tomorrow.

Louisa
We have too much cash in the bank. In what will you invest next?

Oong
I have some real estate in mind.

*(**John** emerges from stage left)*

John
Sir

Oong
Yes, John.

John
Sir, there is a ... Mr. Ar-Kan (?) ... here to see you, sir.

Oong
(Puzzled,)

Ar-Kan?

(Ponders. to himself)

Could it be ...?

*(To **John**)*

Show him in.

*(He crosses to downstage right and anxiously looking at the door wondering whether it is the same **Kan** who worked for his family in Canton.)*

John
(Bows)

Yes sir.

(Walks to the door.)

Mr. Ar Kan, please...

*(**Kan** follows **John** to enter.)*

Kan
*(Knells to greet **Oong**)*

Master, do you remember me? Your servant Ar-Kan.

Oong
*(Recognizes **Kan**. Rushes over to help **Kan** to his feet.)*

Ar-Kan, It's really you? How do you come to be here?

Kan

Oh, it's a long story, master.

Oong

You should not address me as master anymore. We are in America now. America is a democratic country. You should simply address me as Ar showe.

Kan

No master, that would be too rude.

Oong

But I insist.

Kan

I .... I'll try. Good afternoon, Master ... Ha ha ... Mr Oong.

Oong
*(Turns to **Louisa**.)*

Louisa, Ar-Kan and I were from the same village. Ar-Kan used to help my father at the teashop in Canton.

*(To **Ar-Kan**)*

This is my wife Louisa.

Kan
(Bows)
How are you? Mrs. Oong.

Louisa
How are you Mr. ...?

Oong
Liang, Liang Ar Kan.

Louisa
Mr. Liang.
*(She shakes **Kan**'s hand. Then she turns to **Oong**)*
You two old friends haven't seen each other for twenty years now then. Well, I'd better leave you alone to talk about old times. If you would excuse me I am going to tell the cook that we have a guest.

Kan
Oh, thank you, Mrs. Oong.

*(**Kan** bows and smiles. **Louisa** exits from stage right. **Kan** looks around admiringly.)*

Oong
Come. Sit down. I read in the newspaper about the Chinese coming to North Adams. But I didn't expect you to be among them. You must tell me. What have you been doing?

Kan:
(Sighs)
Ai, it's a long story.

Oong
How are your brothers?

Kan
Ah Hong is home with my parents. Ah Lum was killed in San Francisco.

Oong
What?

Kan
(Sobs.)
He was buried alive in a mudslide while building a road.

Oong

NO!!!

Kan

One time when I was grading a street in San Francisco I found a horse and three dead Chinese buried in the mud.

Oong

Good havens!!! Right in the city streets?

Kan

What city? San Francisco was no more than a hamlet then. It was very rough. We filled the marshes with rocks and mud that we move from the hills. And then we built houses on the filled land and terraces cut form the hillsides. We changed the terrain.

Oong

You are like the "Old Fool" in the Chinese fable.

Kan

Exactly. ... Oh. we didn't expect things to be so hard.

Oong

Could you find other jobs?

Kan

Yes, yes, we could have any job that the white people did not want or couldn't do. We built house that were prefabricated in China. We reclaimed swamps. We people from the Pearl River Delta area are well equipped with good techniques for those types of work.

Oong

The Chinese contribute so much to California. Americans should have appreciated you.

Kan

Oh, yes, our employers appreciated us. They said we were diligent and hardworking. .... I also worked in the mines. Coal mines, silver mines, gold mines.... All sorts of mines.

Oong

Oh! gold mine? That sounds profitable. Did you make good money?

Kan

Hardly. Most of us only scratched a living. Because we were only allowed to work for mining companies making twenty some dollars a month. We had to provide our own meals and tents. And we had to pay a very heavy tax that others didn't have to pay.

Oong
Every one has to pay tax.

Kan
But I mean the foreign miners' tax. We Chinese are the only foreign miners.

Oong
Were there miners from other countries?

Oong
Yes. But they were not considered foreigners. Because they are from Europe. They could soon become American citizens. We Chinese are not allowed to be naturalized. So we are the only foreign miners. The tax collectors are brutal. They threatened us with knives and guns. My cousin was killed because he could not satisfy the tax collector's extortion.

Oong
That's outrageous. Such thing can never happen in Massachusetts. America is a democratic country.

Kan
May be.

(Louisa enters from stage left)

Louisa
Gentlemen, pardon me.
(She points at her purse on the table)
I need to get this. Mr. Liang, do you prefer Chinese or European food?

Kan
Oh, Mrs. Oong, thank you. Thank you. Either will be fine.

Louisa
I will have the cook prepare Chinese food for you.

Kan
Thank you.

(Louisa exits)

Kan
She is so kind.

Oong

Yes. She is a fine lady.

Kan

The white men had no one to wash their dirty clothes. So my cousin Wah Lee opened a laundry. The business was so good that more and more opened. Now there are about 2,000 of them in San Francisco.

Oong

Washing dirty clothes all day long. That must be hard.

Kan

Of course. That's why white people didn't want to do it and the Chinese could have the business without much trouble. In other jobs, as soon as the Chinese got a toehold they would be pushed out.

Oong
(Discomfited)

I had no idea ...

Kan

Yes, things were bad there. There were some Americans who were good to us. But the mean ones, oh ... They beat us, kicked us, spit on us right on the street for no reason at all. They robbed us; burned down our houses ...

Oong

Why didn't you appeal to the police?

Kan

The police? The police just looked the other way. The law does not protect us. We were not allowed to testify in court.

Oong
(Riled)

You mean, they just perpetrated those crimes without being punished?

Kan

Hardly. They even threatened our white employers. Last year, six white employers were murdered because they wouldn't fire their Chinese workers. The situation was so bad that some kind-hearted Americans formed a Chinese Protection Committee. And the Six Companies had to hire private police and form their own protective force.

Oong

Six Companies?

Kan

Oh. That's the associated merchants' guild. It's also called the Chinese Consolidated Benevolent Association. You know what? The Americans did not attack the Chinese merchants.

Oong

I suppose it's because the Chinese merchants are not competing for the same market.

Kan

You are right. Also because the merchants have money. It's the same everywhere. Rich people are treated differently. Look how you are treated.

Oong
(Thinks about Scott Collins insulting William)
Ar-Kan, I may have more money, but I am a foreigner, a Chinese, just the same.

Kan

I still think it's not the same. Well, anyway, in 1865, I was recruited by the Central Pacific Railroad Company to build the transcontinental railroad until it was completed last year. 15,000 Chinese were put on the job. We completed the job in half the expected time.

Oong

The newspaper stories did not expatiate on the magnitude of the Chinese participation.

Kan

We did the hardest part of the work. The Sierra Nevada and the Rockies were killing. There were solid granite mountains and gorges. We had to cut on the side of a granite mountain and make a ledge for the railway roadbed. There was no place to stand while we did the job. You know how we did it?

Oong

How?

Kan

We were lowered from above in baskets held by ropes. Suspended in mid air, 1,400 feet above the river. We chipped away the rock with hammers and crowbars.

Oong

Good Heavens!

Kan

Our superintendent said only the Chinese would do such a thing. We were still working in the Sierra Nevada when winter came. That biting cold was more than you could imagine. The ground was frozen solid. And after a storm we had to shovel away 60-foot drifts of snow before we could reach the ground. We dug tunnels between the work site and our living quarters under the surface of the snow. 1,400 Chinese died on the job. Many of them were buried in avalanches. Some were from our home village, Toishan. My cousin Ar-fok ... was ...

(He cries)

*(**Louisa** enters from stage left)*

Louisa

Gentlemen, pardon me again. Dinner is ready...
*(Notices **Kan** crying.)*
Something wrong? Darling, ... is something ... wrong?

Oong
(Emotionally)
Yes, something is very wrong in this world.

Louisa

Dinner ... is ready.

*(**Louisa** exits stage right)*

Oong
(Sighs)
They traveled thousands of miles to find a good life, instead they found death. Have their bones been moved back home?

Kan

No. It would cost too much. And a new city ordinance forbade the moving of the bones.

Oong

Having one's bones buried in his hometown is an age-old Chinese custom. Not allowing that is like not allowing one to go home. That is inhumane.

Kan

There are too many ordinances that make our lives insufferable. I hope one day things will change ... in this democratic country.

Oong
(Opens the money case brought in by John

earlier and takes out a big bag of money. Then he quickly sits down and begins to write a letter.)

How many did you say were buried in San Francisco?

Kan

The official number is 1,400. But ...

Oong

Do you have the address of the Six Companies?

Kan

Yes,

*(Reaches for his pocket and takes out some papers. He picks one out and hands it to **Oong**.)*

Here it is.

Oong

(Takes over the paper and quickly scribbles the address on the envelop. Then he calls his servant.)

John, John

*(**John** enters from stage-left)*

John

Yes, sir.

Oong

Take this to the post office ... This letter and money.
*(He throws the big bag of money to **John**.)*
Hurry. Send by express mail ... To this address.
*(He hands the piece of paper to **John**.)*

John

This is too much money, sir. It's too dangerous to walk with this much ...

Oong

Take my carriage. And hurry up!!! Go!!!

John
(Bows)

Yes, sir.

*(**John** exits)*

Oong

I asked them to send everyone's bones back to his village.

Kan

Oh, Mr. Oong, you are so very kind. The ghosts of the dead and their living family members will be grateful to you forever. Because you have a big heart, Heaven rewards you with good fortune. Look how wealthy you are! You live in such a beautiful house and enjoy such prestige.

Oong

I have been fortunate so far. I was the only Chinese here. People were mostly curious about me at first. When my business prospered they began to accept me. When I generously donated money to charities, they respected me.
(Changes the subject and tone of voice.)
Do you find the atmosphere in North Adams more congenial?

Kan

Oh yes. The townspeople are very friendly, even the union people. They asked us to join their union. We are happy there.

Oong

Maybe Massachusetts is different. Our senator Charles Sumner works very hard to have all the discriminatory laws repealed. This year he introduced two bills proposing that Chinese be granted citizenship and voting rights.

Kan

Your senator speaks for the Chinese? Maybe Massachusetts is really different.

*(**William** enters from stage left)*

William

Good afternoon, father.
*(Notices **Kan**)*

Good afternoon, sir...

Oong
*(Introduces **Kan** to **William**)*

Mr. Liang. He is an old friend of mine.
*(To **Kan**)*

This is my oldest son, William.

William

Pleased to meet you Mr. Liang.

Kan
(Bows)

It's an honor to meet you, Master William.

William
(Unexpected. Smiles)
Master ... ? ah, ha!!

Oong
(To William)
How was your final exam?

William
Father, um ...
(Reluctantly)
final exam ... Father, you may now hire me as your legal attorney!

Oong
(Surprised and happily)
What? Ha, Ha, congratulations, son, I am proud of you. Very proud of you.

William
Pardon me father, I have to go get dressed for the party.

Oong
Is Laurie going?

William
Yes, I am going to pick her up at 7:00.
(Pauses, happily and sincerely)
Father, I love you.

*(**William** looks at **Oong** for a second then exits stage-right.)*

Oong
*(Touched by the son's showing of affection. Lovingly watches **William** hurry off.)*
I love you too, son.

Kan
Mr. Oong, you are a lucky man.

Oong
(Contendly)
Yes, I am. Have you been back home for visits?

Kan
No. I have no money to do that. How about you, Mr. Oong?

Oong
I made a promise to my mother-in-law before I married Louisa that I would not take her to China. I can't break my promise.

Kan
Oh, that's too bad. The honorable Mr. and Mrs. Oong senior have not seen their daughter-in-law?

Oong
(Apparently regretful)
No.

Kan
How many children do you have, Mr. Oong?

Oong
Two daughters and one son. Another son died. How about you?

Kan
Me? I am still single. I suppose your children are allowed to attend public school because Mrs. Oong is a white woman, huh?

Oong
Why?

Kan
In California Chinese children are not allowed to attend school.

Oong
America is a democratic country. How can such things be allowed?

Kan
Unfortunately they are allowed. Do you think things will change for the better?

Oong
May be. But I am afraid changes will not come soon enough.
(Takes out a stack of money from his money case.)
Please accept this gift from me. I hope it will help you start a better life.

Kan
(Moved, declines the gift.)
Oh, Master, I cannot accept this. Please take it back.

Oong

It's only a small amount. If this is not enough, ...

*(Takes out more money and pushes it to **Kan**.)*

Here, take this too.

Kan

(Declining the gift.)

Master, uh, Mr. Oong, thank you. Thank you, But I cannot ... I ...

Oong

Please, Ar Kan. Please give me a chance to do something for you. I feel this is the first time in my life that I am making a meaningful contribution. Things will change. Ar Kan. They have to change.

(Lights off)

SCENE 18, 1876
The Year of the Centennial
Oong Ar-Showe's Gift to the Centennial Celebration

*(**Actors 1, 2, 4** are on stage as the lights at downstage come up. They announce the scene and introduce the characters. At upstage the lights are still off. **Louisa** who has been ill for sometime lounges on a sofa in the dark holding a book in hand.)*

Actor 1

Scene 18, the year of the Centennial

Actor 2

In a sitting room in Oong's home

Actor 4

Characters:

Actor 1

Louisa, Oong Ar-Showe

Actor 2

Mary, now Mrs. Sullivan

Actor 4

Mayor Sullivan, and William

*(The **actors 1, 2** and **4** exit after the announcement. Lights come up in the area where **Louisa** is. **Oong** enters from stage-left and walks toward Louisa.)*

Oong

Hello dear, how are you feeling?

Louisa

Just tired. How did the meeting go?

Oong

It went well.

Louisa

How much did they ask for?

Oong

They did not have a definite budget. The Special Event's Committee made some elaborate plans, not knowing where the money would come from. They formed a Fundraising Committee. They asked if I could contact some friends and interest them to give. You know I wouldn't want to do that. So I just gave them a blank check, so to speak. I said I would pay for the float parade in the morning, the firework display and the torch parade at night, and the banquet and the ball. I guess this would cost about $55,000.

Louisa

Dear, that's a great deal of money!!

Oong

Yes. But this is a very special occasion, the centennial of America's independence. I am glad to sponsor the celebration. Besides, William is graduating from college. We are combining two celebrations in one. William can attend the banquet and go to the ball too. He can take his girl friend.

Louisa

He'll like that. Lizzie and little Louisa will enjoy it enormously too. They were talking about what gowns to buy and what jewelry to wear to the ball already. They are determined to show themselves off. Too bad I cannot do anything. They asked me to chair the committee for the Centennial Ball and Banquet. Where do I have the energy and spirit to do it?

Oong

Dear you shouldn't tire yourself. But you have to keep your spirit up.

Louisa

I am trying. But this illness is getting me down. I am afraid I won't live too long ...

Oong
*(Strides to **Louisa** and holds her hand.)*
Dear, don't think that way. You can't think that way. I need you. My life will be worthless without you.

Louisa

Dear Charles, there is something I must say to you.

Oong

Yes, dear, what is it?

Louisa

I sense that something is troubling you. Your mood is sullen at times. You are not happy. I am worried.

Oong

No, there is nothing.

Louisa

Yes, something must have been troubling you. Is it homesickness? I often felt very sorry that an old promise almost ruined you.

Oong

Dear, a promise is a promise. I don't regret it.

Louisa

Darling, all I ever want is to make you happy. I don't know whether I ...

Oong
*(Cuts short **Louisa**'s words.)*

Dear. I am just about the happiest man on earth.

Louisa
(Tears in her eyes)

I know. You have done everything for me and because of me. I will be grateful to you in my next life too.

Oong

Louisa, don't say that. You know everything I have done, I have done it with great pleasure. I love you.

Louisa

You have made such a big sacrifice leaving your parents behind for this long. I noticed the change in you since your mother passed away six years ago.

Oong

It was not just my mother's death that saddened me so. It is the disturbing news about the Chinese ... the massacres of Chinese in Los Angeles, and similar riots elsewhere. I could not do a thing to help them. Now the boisterous demand of Chinese exclusion has been a hot issue. I can't help identifying myself with the other Chinese. I could have been one of them. We all came from the same district in south China. We are the same people. The only difference is that I have money.

Louisa
(Helplessly)

Ar-Showe

Oong

I often think ...

*(**Mary** enters from stage left and cuts short **Oong**'s words)*

Mary

Hello, Charles. Hi, Louisa dear. How do you feel?

Louisa

Hello.

Mary

I just came back from the Ladies Committee meeting. Everyone regretted that you could not chair the Committee. But Charles, my dear, I hope you can help.

Louisa

Ar-Showe already promised the Special Events Committee that he would pay for everything.

Mary

Oh, that's wonderful. We were discussing about how much to charge the guests. If Charles pays for everything that means the proceeds will be pure profit.

Oong

Yes. Put it aside for your next event.

Mary

Sure, I will remind them not to bother you too often.
*(To **Louisa**)*
You see, Louisa, I can do that but you cannot.

Louisa
(Smiles.)
Have you decided which band to hire?

Mary

Yes. The Clarence Band. You like that band. We will ask them to play your favorite music.

Oong

We may not be there. I don't want Louisa to exert herself.

Louisa

But I would like to go, dear. It's the Centennial Ball. And it may be my last ...

Mary
*(Cuts short **Louisa**'s words)*
It will be everyone's first and last centennial ball!

*(**Butler** enters from stage left)*

Butler
His Honor Mayor Sullivan is here sir.

Mary
Patrick?

*(**Mayor Sullivan** enters from stage left)*

Sullivan
Mrs. Ar-Showe, how are you
*(Kisses **Louisa**'s hand then kisses **Mary** on the check.)*
Hello dear.

Louisa
Hello.

Mary
Hello, dear.

Sullivan
Mr. Ar-Showe, how are you sir?
(He bows.)
I came here to thank you for your great generosity.

Oong
Mayor Sullivan, are you bowing to me?

Sullivan
Huh?

Oong
Yes, you are bowing to me. But the sun has not risen from the west yet.

Sullivan
(Puzzled, then realizes the joke.)
Oh. ho, Mr. Ar-Showe. That ...that was an old joke. Please forgive me ...

Oong
*(Walks up to **Sullivan** and put his arm*

*around **Sullivan**.)*

Tell me, Mayor Sullivan. How well do you know your voters?

Sullivan

Like the back of my hand.

Oong

Well then, you must know how many Chinese voters you have.

Sullivan

Yes.

(He holds out his hand and counts his fingers.)

Eh, one... One. That's you. You are the only one.

Oong

Ah, I see. The one and only!!! Then, I must be the Emperor. That's why you bowed to me. Ha Ha Ha!!

Sullivan

(Embarrassed, laughs uneasily)

Ha! Ha! Ha!.

(Cleans his throat. Changes to a serious tone.)

Uh, Mr. Ar-Showe the City Council and I would like to have a special ceremony on July 4th at which to accept your contribution and to give you an award. This is to show our gratitude and respect for all you have done for the city and its residents through the years.

Oong

Thank you, Mayor Sullivan. But it won't be necessary. I did those things because I enjoyed doing them.

Sullivan

We all know that. Mr. Ar-Showe, you are truly a great man. The world would be a much better one if there were more people like you.

Oong

No, Mayor Sullivan. The world would be a much better one if everyone were tolerant of others, accepted people for what they were and treated them with fairness. Don't you think so?

Sullivan

Yes, yes, of course.

(He is ready to leave.)

Please excuse me.

*(To **Mary**)*
Dear ...

*(During the last exchanges of conversation **Mary** stands up to look herself in the mirror, straightening out her skirt and hat. She is not paying attention to **Louisa** or the two men. **Louisa** is feeling very ill. She faintly calls out to **Oong** '"Darling!" No one hears her. "Darling!!" She calls for the second time when **Oong** was giving his final speech to **Sullivan**. Still no one hears her. She struggles to stand up, walks a few steps toward **Oong** and **Sullivan**. She collapses on the floor. Everyone is shocked. **Oong** drops himself on the floor beside her. **Mary** also bent over **Louisa**.)*

Oong
Louisa, Darling ...

*(He holds her up. At this time **William** joyfully calls his mother before he enters)*

Louisa
I wish to let you know that those strolls in the park are most enjoyable to me.

Oong
Darling, these are ...
(Cries)
Darling----

William
(Off stage, joyfully,)
Mother, mother,
*(**William** enters the stage carrying a few gift boxes.)*
I brought you these...
*(He sees the scene, shocked, drops the boxes on the floor; he rushes toward **Louisa**.)*
Mother, Mother ... Get the doctor! Get the doctor!!
*(**Sullivan** rushes off to get the doctor)*
Oh, God!!!

(Lights off)

SCENE 19
The Year of the Centennial
Congressional Hearing

*(As the lights come up **Actors 1, 4** are on stage narrating the scene.)*

Actor 1

Scene 19, 1876

Actor 4

Congressional hearing

Actor 1

In 1876 in the heat of the anti-Chinese sentiment, California's legislature formed a committee to investigate the issue of Chinese immigration. Appointed to the committee were all anti-Chinese advocates.

Actor 4

The 42 individuals who testified in front of the Committee were also anti-Chinese radicals. A report of their findings was made public and was sent to the Federal Government.

Actor 1

U.S. Senator Oliver P. Morton from Indiana suggested that the Congress should also investigate the problem. A Congressional Special Committee was thus formed.

Actor 4

The six member Committee conducted hearings with 129 people which resulted in 1,200 pages of testimonies.

Actor 1

Morton was seriously ill and could not participate in the writing of the final report. In the end, a five-page report was written by Senators Cooper, Sargent and Piper, all anti-Chinese enthusiasts. Morton's own notes, a fair assessment that was published after his death, were not reviewed by the Congress.

Actor 4

Characters:

Actor 5
(Announces the character he plays)

Senator Cooper of Tennessee

Actor 2
(Announces the character he plays)
Senator Sargent of California

Actor 1
(Announces the character he plays)
Senator Piper also of California

Actor 2
Two other committee members, Senator Meads of New York and Senator Wilson of Massachusetts were absent.

Actor 4
The scene takes place in a conference room in the state house.

*(**Actor 4** exits. The others assume their characters. The stage is dark. The area with the conference table and the three senators is lit. The testifiers stand in the dark. A spot light shines on whoever is speaking at the time.)*

Piper
Shall we hear Governor Low's testimony? He is a former congressman and a U.S. Minister to China as well as a former Governor of California. His view on Chinese immigration would be somewhat valuable. What did he say about the building of the railroad?

Cooper
(Leafs through his papers)
Oh yes, I got it right here. He said: "The Central Pacific Railroad company employed 80-90% Chinese workers to build the transcontinental railroad ...

Piper
What did he say about the white laborers?

Cooper
He said that if they had hired white laborers, it would have taken longer to build because white laborers were hard to come by and the job would have been put off. And it would have cost a lot more.

Piper
Why is that?

Cooper
Because, he said, the white laborers were paid $45 a month and the company had to provide their meals. The Chinese laborers were paid $31 a month and they supplied their own meals. This saved the Company 5 million dollars.

Sargent
(Mumbles his objections to these remarks)

Piper
Did he say anything else?

Cooper
He said the Chinese had enriched the California state treasury about $900 million a year. That equaled the total income derived from the mines in California, Nevada and Dakota. The Chinese laborers in railroad building and tule land reclamation had augmented the state's wealth by 289 million 700 thousand dollars.

(**Piper** is very impatient in hearing these reports.)

Piper
*(Interrupts **Cooper**.)*
Well I don't think we need to hear anymore testimonies like that. We have enough information to write our report.

Cooper
Shall we call Senator Meads of New York and Senator Wilson of Massachusetts to discuss it?

Piper
Well, I don't think we'll have to do that. Senator Meads never shows up and Senator Wilson never wants to do the work. With Morton being sick, the duty of writing the report to the congress is on our shoulders.

Sargent
It's just as well. I think the three of us have the same view on this issue.

Cooper
That is true. How do we proceed with the task?

*(**Sargent** is about to say something. But **Piper** preempts him. **Sergeant** shrugs his shoulder.)*

Piper
(Walks to the desk and puts his hand on the piles of paper.)
The testimonies have been separated into three classes. Those giving the strongest evidence on why the Chinese must be excluded are in Class One. Those having the opposite view are in Class Two. The third are those not having opinions. 40% of those who testified belong to Class One.

Cooper

How many are in Class Two?

Sargent

52%.

Cooper

That high?!

Sargent

Well it doesn't matter. We will base our report on the 40%.

Piper

Should we review some of the testimonies. After listening to 129 people, I don't remember too much.

Sargent

Of course.

*(He picks up some paper from one pile and hands it to **Cooper**, and again some to **Piper**. He takes some himself.)*

Ha, listen to this one: This is from a spokesman of the City of San Francisco. He says: "The reasons why we are anti-Chinese are (1) they are in direct conflict with the welfare of our laborers. ...

Piper
(Interrupts him)

Yes. we know that. Next.

Sargent
(Reads from a piece of paper)

This one says: "They are heathens who cannot be converted to Christians. They are dangerous to society. Their depraved culture will affect our people to be immoral as they are. They will always be a class of scurrilous laborers, without education, not caring about America." This one says "Their faces are inexpressive. Their queues are like pigs' tails. Their clothing is ugly. They transport things with shoulder poles. They do not speak fluent English." And this one says: "They did not come to become American citizens or because they were politically oppressed in China. They came just to make money. China's population is many times larger than that of America. If we do not ban their immigration America will become a province of China. They do not adopt our way of life. There are 13 Buddhist temples in Chinatown. Such temples should not be allowed in our Christian nation."

Piper

Well said. But we know that too. Next.

Cooper
(Reading from a piece of paper)
And, "They did not bring their wives and children along. The women who have come are all prostitutes. They do not buy property. They are useless to America. Their Six Companies is an underground government. It has a court, a detention center and a jail inside its building. They take the law in their own hands. All Chinese laborers are slaves."

Piper
This is from Mr. Frank Pixley, a representative of the San Francisco City government. Frank says
(Reading from a piece of paper)
"The population of Chinese in California almost equals the white voting population. If they were given voting rights, they would control every election. Their population growth is faster than that of the others combined. We find that our territory on the Pacific Coast will soon be occupied entirely by that foreign race. This serious situation must be checked."
(Flipping through more papers)
These express mostly the same sentiment. We will write the report based on these and have a strong case.

Cooper
Shall we review some from the other side?

Piper
Ha, ha. What's the point of doing that? We are not going to quote them in our report, are we? Ha ha ha. Our duty is to collect evidence on why the Chinese must be excluded. It is not our intention to find out how much the Chinese have contributed to California or the nation.

(lights off)

SCENE 20
Returning to China, 1878

*(**Oong** and **William** are in an area of the stage not illuminated. The downstage where the narrators stand is lit. The narrators are **actors #1** and **#4**.)*

Actor 4

Scene 20,

Actor 1

1878, Ar-Showe returns to China

Actor 4

Characters: William, Oong Ar-Showe, Mary

Actor 1

In the drawing room of Oong's home.

*(**Actors 4** and **1** exit. Lights up where **Oong** and **William** are.)*

William

Father, Are you serious? You are going to leave us here and go to China?

Oong

William. This is a very hard decision. It is not without a great deal of conflict in my heart.

William

Why do you have to go? You have been here all your life.

Oong

No, William, not all my life. I was about your age, well, one year older than you are now when I came here. It's been 28 years. Long enough. I should be going home.

William

But this is your home.

Oong

Yes, in a way. I had your mother. And I have you and your sisters. This should be my home. But now, your mother is gone. Lizzie is married. Little Louisa is 17. You are all grown up. I have no more worry. And there is no reason for me to stay anymore.

William

But father, people don't just suddenly decide to leave everything and go to China.

Oong

But William, China is my country. China is where my home used to be.

William

Then, why didn't you go before?

Oong

Because I made a promise to Grandmother.

William

What did you promise her?

Oong

I promised her that I would never take your mother to China with me.

William

You never told me that. I always thought this was where you belonged. I seldom think about China, that very far away place about which we know very little.

Oong

William, I am sorry. I should have taught you about China.

William

Why did you promise Grandmother that you would not take mother to China?

Oong

That was before your mother and I were married. In fact it was when I went to Grandmother and Grandfather's house to ask for your mother's hand. They were reluctant to allow me to marry your mother.

William

Because you were from China?

Oong

Exactly. They didn't know anything about China. It was a far away place, like you just said. They couldn't imagine letting their daughter be taken to such an unknown, far away place.

William

So you promised them never to take her there. And you never went back.

Oong

That's right.

William

Did you think about going back? Did you want to go back?

Oong

Of course, often, very much.

William

But you didn't. Because of a promise. What a sacrifice!

Oong

No. I don't regard it as a sacrifice. A promise is a promise. You know. We Chinese value our words above anything.

William

Now that mother is gone you are not bound by your promise any more.

Oong

That is not the reason. The pain of losing your mother is too deep. This house, this town, everything here reminds me of her. But this is not the only reason.

William

Of course, things are never so simple.

Oong

No. Especially not in my case. William, I am a Chinese living in America. I left my parents behind and never went home. To a Chinese, this is most unfilial. I neglected my duty as a son. Now, as a father, I am about to leave my children behind and go to China. To an American, this is most unfatherly. I have failed to be a good son and I am failing to be a good father.

William

Oh father!

Oong

All my life, what have I accomplished? Nothing. I made a lot of money. That's all. To the Chinese, merchants are not in a respected class. I have given a lot of money to benefit the public. But I am not able to do a thing for my own compatriots.

William

You gave them money too. Didn't you? You went to North Adams to see them and invite some of them here. They came to mother's funeral. They told me how wonderful you were.

Oong

Oh, that's nothing. That was not what I meant. I meant I was not able to alleviate the hardship for them. Every time I read about how much they are hated, despised, how much they are unwanted, I feel guilty.

William

Feel guilty? Why? Father, I don't understand.

Oong

My feelings are complex. I ... I feel that I have betrayed my countrymen. They have suffered cruel treatment in my adopted country whereas I have enjoyed prestige and privileges. When my adopted country infracts an international treaty, I mean the Burlingham Treaty, I feel that I cannot escape the blame either.

William

But leaving the country wouldn't help.

Oong

I know it wouldn't help. But I can dispose of some of that guilt. I will warn the people in Canton about coming to America. I will tell them that it is better to be desperate at home than to be beaten, humiliated, even killed in a foreign country. This is not a place for them. It is not a place for me either. I don't belong here. A Chinese will never become an American. He is a foreigner forever.

William

But father, everyone highly respects you. People are proud to be associated with you.

Oong

(Sad and ireful)
It's my money. I bought my way to where I am.

William

Things will change, father. I am sure things will change for the better for the Chinese immigrants.

Oong

I am afraid it will become worse before it will be better. I am afraid I will not see the change in my lifetime.

William
Father, if you must go, take me with you. I want to go to China with you.

Oong
Son, China is not a place for you. You are half an American. You will not be accepted there. People may not mistreat you but they will not take you as one of their own. Stay. Your sisters may need you.

William
(Dejected)
Father, are you ever going to come back here?

Oong
Probably not.

(**Mary** *Enters from stage left.*)

Mary
Charles,
*(To **William**)*
Hi, William.

William
Hello, Aunt Mary.

Oong
Hi.

Mary
Everything is well planned. The farewell party will be held at David Ayer's house. This is the draft of the invitation to you. They did not know that I got hold of a copy. I can't resist showing it to you beforehand.
*(Handing it to **Oong**)*
Do you want to read it?
(Changes her mind.)
No, I'll read it to you:

(*While **Mary** is reading the invitation **Oong** slowly puts on his Chinese robe.*)

"Mr. Charles Ar-Showe, Maplewood, Oct. 19th, 1878. Dear Sir: At a meeting held at the residence of A.J. Freeman, a committee consisting of Francis Hinckley, George H. Heseltine, James F. Eaton and A.J. Freeman, was appointed to effect arrangements for tendering you a farewell, previous to your departure for China. Those arrangements having been completed, I am instructed by that committee to extend to you a cordial invitation to meet your friends at the residence of Mr. David Ayers, on Wednesday evening, Oct. 23rd. The citizens of Maplewood are desirous of such an opportunity of expressing to you in a measure at least, the appreciation of your characteristics, and their esteem and affection for you personally. Your big-heartedness, public spirit and generosity have endeared you to this town. You have been a resident for many years, and have a host of friends, all hoping you have a pleasant and prosperous visit to your native country, and a safe and not far distant return to this, the one of your adoption. I have the honor to be your most obedient servant. A. J. Freeman, Secretary of the Committee."

Oong
They are very kind.

Mary
The next day they will accompany you to New York to see you off.

William
"A safe and not far distant return," father, didn't they know that you were not coming back?

Mary
(Surprised)
Not coming back? Charles, this is your home.

*(**Oong** steps downstage. The lights become brighter and brighter as he speaks.)*

Oong
My name is Oong Ar-Showe. My name is Oong Ar-Showe. My name is Oong Ar Showe!!!

*(**All the actors** enter from stage right and stage left.)*

All actors
His name is Oong Ar-Showe.

The End

Doris C.J.Chu

AMERICA, AMERICA
a four act play

This work is fully protected by copyright law/ No deletions, substitutions, or alterations may be made by anyone for performance or otherwise without written consent of the author and publisher. No part of this work may be reproduced, translated, transmitted electronically or mechanically, or stored in any information retrieval system, r adapted for film television or t\radio without the prior written consent form the author and publisher of this book.

CAUTION
The performing rights (including public reading) to this play belong exclusively to International Society. Amateur and professional theatre groups alike must acquire written permission and pay royalty to International Society before this work may be staged or read whether or not the performing group is for profit or not-profit, and whether or not admission is charged. International Society via email: info@internationalsociety.us

Printed in the United State of America
All rights reserved

LCC 99-072494
ISBN 1-928730-04-3

Premiere production Cast

Deng Fang-ying	Tina Sooho
Zhao Nan-shan	Edward Gong
Ho Pei-hua	Cynthia Zhu
Li Yong	Victor K. Ng
Liang Mei-lan	Julie K. Hsieh

Estimated running time: two hours

Sets: One unit set--The interior of a room. In the first two acts the room is an office of the International Foundation. In the remaining two acts the room is an artist's studio. The change can be easily achieved by changing the furniture, window dressing and art work decorating the room.

Deng Fang-Ying--A young woman from Taiwan studying art in a college and work-studies at International Society. Later in the play she is a full time artist.
Liang Mei-Lan--a highly popular movie star/pop singer/dancer from China. She is resourceful and shrewd in trying to realize her many dreams l.
Li Yong--an actor from China, currently attending college in Boston studying acting. His becomes a dedicated actor later in the play.
Zhao Nan-Shan--a man from China full of ambitions. Failed to become rich and successful in U.S. China trade he settled for an average life.
Ho Pei-Hua-a young woman from Taiwan, a law student of a college in Boston. After graduation she practices law.

ACT ONE

In an office of the International Foundation. One afternoon in 1985
At Rise: Fang Ying is doing paper work at her desk. Nan Shan pops his head in.

Nan: Hi.

Fang: (*Lift her head from the paper work*) Yes, what can I do for you?

Nan: Oh, nothing. I mean, ah...Are you from Taiwan?

Fang: Yes.

Nan: Ah...I'm from Beij... I mean Peking.

Fang: (*Smiles*) Oh, Mainland China.

Nan: Yes. May I talk with you a little bit? (*Walks toward Fang's desk.*)

Fang: Sure. Please have a seat.

Nan: (*Sits down.*) You work here? Are you the boss?

Fang: (*Smiles*) Yes, I work here. No, I am not the boss.

Nan: (*Extends his hand to Fang*) My name is Zhao Nan-Shan.

Fang: (*Takes his hand and shakes it.*) Deng Fang-Ying.

Nan: I passed by this building many time. I saw some Chinese coming in and out and was curious about this place. What do you do here?

Fang: You mean me personally or this place?

Nan: Both, I guess.

Fang: This is International Foundation, an institution focusing on international cultural exchange and that type of thing. I'm a work-study here. (*Pauses for half a second*) I do a little of everything, mostly helping out.

Nan: What is a work-study?

Fang: Oh, a college student who works part time and being paid partly by the school and partly by the employer. Actually the government subsidizes the school on their share of the pay.

Nan: (*Understood*) Oh---. Why do you want to work while still in school? I don't think it's for the money.

Fang: (*Chuckles*) Why not? That's exactly why I work.

Nan: You people from Taiwan are rich. Why don't your parents support you?

Fang: (*Smiles.*) Not everyone in Taiwan is rich. My parents are pretty well to do though. (*Pause.*) But they don't want to support me.

Nan: (*Puzzled.*) Why?

Fang: Because I did not listen to them. I didn't study what they wanted me to.

Nan: What did they tell you to study?

Fang: Medicine, engineering,....One of those "useful" subjects. But I insisted that I wanted to study art. And they said: "Why study that useless thing? You will starve to death and we will not help you to reach the dead end." Since they are so adamant and I am stubborn...

Nan: (*Cuts short Fang's sentence.*) You have to earn your own living.

Fang: You got it.

Nan: In China, artists make more money than doctors and engineers. It's not so here?

Fang: No. Over here, an artist may starve. But of course it depends on the artist himself. If he is famous he can sell a lot of work at very high prices. The competition is extremely keen. Some very good artists still don't make it. Medical doctors and engineers have pretty straight forward paths. Their incomes are predictable. Of course there are better ways for an artist to make money too--the commercial way. But I am not interested in that.

Nan: In that case I think your parents are right. They gave you good advice--- for your own good. You should have listened to them.

Fang: (*Laughs, amused.*) You just walked in here. A total stranger. And you side with my parents? You sound like a big brother.

Nan: I just think they are right. Unless you have some great plan that will make you rich.

Fang: What do you study?

Nan: No, I am not in school. I've been here for only three months. This is a very different place from China. Too much freedom. You don't know what to do with it.

Fang: (*Perplexed.*) Not in school? How did you come here? I thought that only students were allowed to leave China and come here. My classmate from China told me that. Not so?

Nan: Usually it is so. But in my case... well, I am an immigrant.

Fang: (*curiously*) Immigrant? How?

Nan: I have a cousin. She brought me here..

Fang: Oh. But you don't go to school?

Nan: (*Sighs.*) Ai! I can't. You know. What school do I go to? Graduate school? College? Or high School?

Fang: (*Puzzled*) High school?

Nan: Right. I had only one year of junior high. (*Fang is more puzzled. She waits for Nan Shan to continue.*) The Cultural Revolution. You must have heard of the Cultural Revolution. Haven't you?

Fang: Of course, everybody has.

Nan: The Cultural Revolution interrupted my education. I joined the Red Guard.

Fang: (*Curiously*) You were a Red Guard? I heard the Red Guards ran around trying to destroy China's cultural legacies.

Nan: That was a crazy time. We thought we were doing the right thing, not knowing we were ruining the country and ourselves.

Fang: But I heard that after the Cultural Revolution schools re-opened and college education was highly valued.

Nan: Absolutely. But there were millions of people knocking on the door and only the younger ones with "clean family background" got to go. I was 23, too old to be admitted. My grandfather on my mother's side owned land before the Liberation so my background was labeled as one of the "Five Blacks."

Fang: "Five Blacks!" I've heard that expression before. (*Jestingly*) Being a Red Guard didn't change you to "Red?"

Nan: (*Seriously*) No way. (*Sighs.*) I belong to a generation of sacrificed souls. China ruined me. I have no future there. But America is a land of opportunities. That's why I came.

Fang: I'm sure you will find a lot of opportunities here. But I think being a foreigner and without a college degree won't get you too far.

Nan: (*Debates*) I heard that in America you can succeed in anything you want...

Fang: (*Interrupts Nan. Jokingly*) And you agreed with my parents that I should not study art!

Nan: (*Ignores Fang's remark.*) ...and I want to be rich and successful. (*dreaming*) I want to do big business, ..international trade.... between China and America... I can help both countries. I will be the bridge. I can help America sell cutting edge technology to China, ...and weapons.

Fang: Weapons?

Nan: (*excitedly*) Yes. Don't you know., America has the state of the art weapons, just what China needs?

Fang: (*not taking him seriously*) I don't know. I don't think that's something you, a private individual, can do. It's between the governments. Selling weapons! I think you'd better try to get into some school. That's more practical.

Nan: But that's too slow. There are plenty of Chinese, like you people from Taiwan and Hong Kong, they go to school, get Ph.D. What do they do? They are college professors, medical doctors, engineers. That's all. They don't make big money. Yes, may be Dr. An Wang is an exception. We got to find short cuts. Smart people take the short cuts.

Fang: I have not heard of such talk from anyone. Chinese people value education. No matter what they will do later they must get their education first. My uncle was very handsome and talented in acting when he was younger. One time a film producer from Hong Kong spotted him and offered him a contract to play lead in several films. The pay was very good, of course. My grandparents told him that he had to finish college and graduate school before he could become a movie star.

Nan: That is foolish. Hong Kong movie stars make a lot of money and they don't need college education. Why must your uncle finish graduate school to do that?

Fang: Just because my grandparents thought education was more important than anything else.

Nan: What movies is your uncle in? May be I have seen some of them.

Fang: He is not in any of them. He is a professor now.

Nan: How much does he make? Not very much. I don't think. You see, that is the beaten path your uncle and most other Chinese have taken. It doesn't take imagination and there is no risk, no excitement. The result is so predictable. You don't lose and you don't win big.

Fang: We are not talking gambling here.

Nan: But life is gambling. If I don't gamble what do I do with an elementary school education.

Fang: (*humorously*) May be you can become a movie star.

Nan: (S*miles*) I don't have any acting talent and I haven't got any offer.

Fang: Then, your best bet is still going to school. How's your English?

Nan: (S*hakes his head*) I don't know any English.

Fang: I thought not. Not knowing English, not having any special skill, not familiar with the society and the systems. You don't have much of a chance.

Nan: I am intelligent. Since I don't waste any time in school like the others I am ahead of them by many years. I can start a career now and they have to wait until they get out of school.

Fang: (*Disagrees*) You must learn English before you can do anything.

Nan: That I do agree. I am going to enroll in an English class. Where should I go? Do you have any suggestions?

Fang: Oh, the International Foundation has an English-as-a-second-language program designed to help new immigrants like you. There are also other places with such program. As a minority you will find various government programs useful to you.

Nan: (S*tunned*) Minority? We are the great Han people, the Chinese! How can we be a minority.

Fang: (*Laughs.*) But we are a minority in America.

Nan: (*Seriously*) We are the majority in the world.

Fang: That's true. But we are still a minority in America.

Nan: (*Gives up; Shakes his head.*)

(*Li Yong and Pei-Hua enter from stage left*)

Pei: Hi, Fang Ying.

Li: Fang Ying.

Fang: (*Looks at Li and Pei*) You know each other?

Pei: No, I don't know him. We just happen to be here at the same time. (*She smiles and takes a glance at Li noticing his apparent good looks.*)

Li: Yea, I had the good fortune to be here at this time to meet this charming young lady.

Fang: Oh (*introduces the three people, points to each one*) Ho Pei Hua, Li Yong. And this is Zhao Nan Shan.

Li: (*Nods*) Oh, Miss Ho. (*turns to Nan and shakes his hand*). How're you doing? (*to Fang, referring to Nan*) We already met at a gathering.

Nan: (*to Li, responding to his greeting*) I am fine. Thank you. (*Turns to face Pei*) How are you?.

Fang: (*to Li*) Any good news?

Li: No. I went to that agency in New York, without an appointment. I gave them my headshot and resume. And I forced my monologue on them. They didn't let me sing or dance. And said to me. "Go home and study English. Come back in two years."

Fang: Oh---. But you already did a couple of plays here. They didn't think your English was adequate?

Li: I acted in college and community productions. This is Broadway.

Pei: (*interested*) Broadway? You are going to be on Broadway? How neat.

Li: Yea, I hope to be on Broadway.

Pei: I envy people in the theatre. And I admire actors. If I had a choice...

Fang: (*Interrupts Pei*) Pei Hua, you could have had a choice but you gave it up.

Pei: What do you mean I gave it up? I didn't have the choice.

Fang: That's because you were too obedient a daughter. (*to Nan Shan*) Here is another example. (*to Pei*) I was telling Nan Shan about my uncle.

Nan: (t*o Pei*) Your parents want you to finish graduate school before becoming an actress, right?

Fang: Worse. Her parents did not allow her to enter that field. And she obeyed.

Pei: Oh, Fang Ying!

Fang: (*Ignores Pei Hua's objection.*) She's going to be a lawyer. We were classmates in Taiwan, you know.

Pei: My parents were not so wrong. Theatre is a very tough field. For an Asian to get on Broadway, that's almost impossible. I don't think I can ever make it. (*to Li Yong*) Where were you from?

Li: Shanghai.

Pei: (*Opens her eyes widely in amazement.*) Shanghai? I can never believe it. You don't look like someone from Shanghai.

Nan: (*Smiles*) I am from Beijing.

Li: (*Feels a little offended*) What does someone from Shanghai look like?

Pei Well, the way you dress and carry yourself, you just don't look like a Mainlander.

Li: Should I take that as a compliment? I suppose to the Taiwanese us Mainlanders are all country bumpkins, awkward, clumsy, poor and filthy.

Nan: (*Smiles, casually*) That is a common notion. That's how the Taiwanese think of the Mainlanders.

Pei: Who is Taiwanese? We were born in Taiwan. That's all. Our parents moved to Taiwan. The local Taiwanese call us Mainlanders

Li: So you are a country bumpkin too.

Fang: Oh, stop that bantering. We are all Chinese.

Li: (*to Pei*) Sorry.

Fang: We are pathetic. In Taiwan we are called Mainlanders. Over here the Mainlanders call us Taiwanese. The Americans call us Chinese. When we go to Taiwan or the Mainland, we are called "The-One-from-American." What are we? Where do we belong?

Pei: (*Ignores Fang's question, still thinking about Li's earlier, sarcastic remark*) So sensitive! I'm sorry too. I guess I'd better leave before I offend more people. .

Li: (*Sincerely*) Please, don't leave on my account. I apologize for being so rude. Really. I should have thanked you for you compliment.

Pei: (*Glances at Li, still annoyed.*) I hope you won't be so sensitive anymore.

Fang: (*to Li*) Which play will you try out for?

Li: M. Butterfly.

Pei: (*Can't help but be interested.*) Oh. Song Li-ling's role? (*Says the wrong thing again*) No. You don't look the part. You are not feminine enough.

Li: Not feminine enough? I am not feminine, period. But I can play it. (*He delivers lines from M. Butterfly.*) "France, France is a country living in the modern era, may be even ahead of it. China is a nation whose soul is deeply rooted two thousand years in the past. What I do, even pouring this tea for you now, has implications."

Fang: (*Claps her hands*) Bravo!

Li: Earlier this year, at the University's Anniversary Celebration, I recited Martin Luther King's "I have a Dream" speech. (*He recites a paragraph from that speech*) "It is a dream deeply rooted in the American dream that one day this nation will rise up and live up the true meaning of its creed. We hold this truth to be self evident that all man are created equal." (*Everyone applauds*) The Boston Globe reported that it was the highlight of the day long event. I only knew a few simple words in that speech. Every other word I had to check the dictionary for its meaning and pronunciation.

Fang: And how about your role as Romeo. (*to the others*) He played Romeo at the Stanford Theatre. That was so wonderful.

Nan: (*not knowledgeable in theatre, but has heard of Romeo and Juliet before. to himself*) Romeo and Juliet.

Li: I didn't understand a single line of it. But I read the Chinese translation. Otherwise I wouldn't know what I was saying.

Pei: (*Gets more interested.*) Who played Juliet? Was she a Chinese too?

Li: No, She was a Caucasian. I was the only Chinese actor in the cast.

(*Nan Shan does not fit in the conversation so he sits in a chair and begins to flip through a magazine.*)

Pei: (*totally impressed*) Wow! That's neat! Too bad I didn't know about it or I would have gone. Were you already an actor in Shanghai?

Li: I was an actor since age eleven. No, No, Correction. I was picked by Beijing Opera Company at eleven. I went to watch my friends audition. I ended up being picked and they were not. Years later I was accepted by Shanghai Drama Institute. After graduation, I taught there. At the same time I acted in a good number of major productions.

Pei: (*curiously*) Your parents were not against your choice? They let you quit school?

Li: In Mainland China, the parents have no say in the children's careers. The government and fate do. My parents belong to the ignominious Five Blacks...

Fang: (*Cuts Li short*) You too?

Li: (*not quite understands what Fang meant*) Yes.

Fang: Nan Shan's parents are also among the "Five Blacks."

Li: Many people are. If you are not from the class of the soldiers, peasants and workers you would likely be one of the Five Blacks. Then you would be doomed. My father was a professor at that time. We had relatives abroad. That made us one of the Five Blacks. I was sent to help build roads at age ten. When I was eleven, Beijing Opera Company sent for the other kids in my work unit to audition. I was not being called but I went to watch. The comrade in the Opera Company sort of liked me. He asked me to sing a song. I did. It was a song I learn while building the road. They thought I was good and told me to stay. I was lucky.

Pei: (*Enthused*) That is fascinating. From a little road builder to a Peking opera singer to a Broadway actor.

Li: I was not really a Beijing Opera singer. I did the martial arts roles, a lot of tumbling and somersaults because my voice changed at age fourteen and could no longer sing soprano and play the female roles I studied for.

Fang: (*to Pei*) These guys from the Mainland, every one has an interesting story to tell. Their lives have many incredible turns. Ours seem so boring. (*Tells a story*) This tenor, Zhou Bin, ---he has a tremendous voice, you have to listen to him sing.--- He said his troupe,---They called it Central Song and Dance Troupe. What an ugly name!---He said the Troupe sent singers and dancers to perform for the peasants and solders. He was trained to sing Chinese art songs and Western opera. The peasants and soldiers didn't appreciate that. He was always inserted, as an extra, between the more welcomed folk dances and fold songs. The audience always shouted at him: "Get off, get off." He couldn't because it was his job to entertain the audience and if he didn't finish his program he would be punished by the leader of the Troupe. So he continued to sing. And the audience threw cabbage and turnip at him. (*Everyone laughs*.)

Li: That was not a joke. I've seen similar things many times.

Fang: Honestly. I cannot stand the way they sing the folk songs. Why do they squeeze the voice from the throat like that? (*She mimics the way the folk song singers sing.*) It is unbearable.

Pei: I can't stand it either.

Li: (*Smiles*) That was a style deliberately created during the Jiang Qing era, you know, Chairman Mao's wife, to mark a distinctive identity for Chinese vocal music.

Nan: (*Defensively*) That style is perfect for the Chinese folk songs.

Pei: But Mei Lan doesn't sing that way.

Li: Mei Lan is not a folk song singer. She sings popular songs, in the styles of those Taiwanese and Hong Kong pop singers. (*changes the subject, to Pei*) What branch of the law do you specialize in?

Pei: Corporate law. Boring stuff. Law is boring.

Li: In America you need a lawyer for everything.

Fang: I heard this joke ...

Pei: I know what you are going to say, Fang Ying. But don't say it.

Fang: (*Ignores Pei-hua*) Lawyers are like sperms. Only one in five million may be a human. (*Everyone laughs.*)

Pei: (*to Li*) She hates lawyers.

Fang: Li Yong, you are coming Saturday, right? I mean to my party. (*to Nan*) If you are interested, Nan Shan, I have some Mainlander friends over this Saturday, consider yourself invited.

Nan: Oh, I'd love to go. What is your address.

Fang: (*Crosses to her desk, takes out a sheet of paper from a drawer and hands it to Nan*) Here, it's the direction. My address and phone number are on it. (*Nan takes it from Fang and looks at it.*)

Pei: (*to Fang*) Fang Ying, you did not invite me.

Fang: Didn't I? Sorry. Of course you are invited.

Li: I'm afraid I can't go. I have this script... I'm working on this script.

Fang: What script? M Butterfly?

Li: (*Smiles.*) No, no. My own script, the one I am writing.

Pei: (*very interested*) You are a playwright too?

Li: I am writing a film script.

Fang: Li Yong, relax. One evening won't kill you. You work too hard.

Pei: (*to Li*) What is the story about?

Li: It's about Lue Gim Gong, a Chinese man in America around the turn of the century. I've done some research on him, an interesting guy. He started as a shoemaker in North Adams, Massachusetts at the same time he worked for a woman, Miss Burlingham, as a gardener. Later on Burlingham took him to Florida. There, this man developed a typed of orange which could endure much lower temperature then other oranges could. He was awarded a medal by the Horticulture Society. I hope to play this character too. I am going to portray him as a real Chinese man. Not the stereo-typed Chinaman in Hollywood's films. You know what I mean.

Nan: Hollywood movies distort the Chinese image so badly. I resent that so much. We should show them what we are really like.

Pei: (*to Li Yong*) I know exactly what you mean. The essence of an ideal Chinese man, the attractiveness, the subtle masculinity, the depth of feelings, the inner strength, none of that has ever been captured in the Hollywood films.

Li: I wish to inject a correct and positive image of the Chinese male into the American films. Starting from this one I am writing.

Pei: Are you writing it for Hollywood? In English?

Li: I cannot write it in English yet. My English is no good. No. This script is in Chinese. When I am done I will have a qualified writer to translate it into English. Or, in a year or so my English may be good enough for me to translate it myself.

Nan: One can really learn that much English in an year?

Fang: (*Ignores Nan's question*) By then the film is made already.

Li: (*Smiles. Takes it as a joke*) yea, right.

Fang: (*to Li*) So, are you coming?

Li: All right, I will come.

Pei: Fang Ying, why do you not ask me to some of your parties? I always ask you to my activities.

Fang: Only a few times I didn't ask you.

Pei: But why? Because you don't want me to mingle with your Mainlander friends?

Fang: Nonsense. You are mingling with them already, here. Why wouldn't I want you to mingle with them?

Pei: You have many Mainlander friends-- artists, musicians --all those interesting people, I haven't met.

Fang: May be subconsciously I thought you and they had very little in common so you would not be very interested in meeting them.

Pei: What do you mean "very little in common?" We speak the same language--We speak Mandarin, don't we?. We are the same race. We have the same five thousand years of history. What do you mean "very little in common?"

Nan: (*Smiles*) Very good. (*Li also smiles and nods his head.*)

Fang: Some Mainlanders and those from Taiwan have prejudice against each other. It's stupid. But they don't see it that way.

Pei: So you were afraid that I was a bigot.

Fang: All right, my fault. I didn't mean that. What I meant was our societal, economic backgrounds were different. That's all.

Pei: (*to Fang*) What do you mean "our?" You are close to them and you don't let me meet them.

Fang: (*Gives up*) Oh, Pei Hua!

Li: Different backgrounds would create different attitudes. That's inevitable. When the kids from Taiwan come here to go to school their parents often come with them and buy houses and new cars for them. On the other hand, we Mainland Chinese students come here with only $50 in our pockets. The first practical problem is how to survive. It's natural for the newly arrived Mainland students to think of the Taiwan kids as spoiled, flaunting their money, high-blown. And it is true that the Taiwan kids often look down upon us Mainlanders. (*to Pei*) You had ten years of English before you came, right? Most of us Mainlanders had none. We couldn't follow the class in the beginning. That's understandable. But these Taiwan kids thought of us as being dumb.

Pei: How do you take classes without knowing English?

Nan: I wonder.

Li: Extremely difficult. Many of us always answered all the questions from the professor with an "yes." That can lead to a whole lot of trouble. A friend of mine, who played the clarinet at the BU orchestra. One time the conductor ask the students to have one more rehearsal before the concert. The professor asked my friend if he understood what he had said. My friend nodded and said "yes." In fact he didn't understand a word. So his missed the rehearsal and the concert. Can you imagine how angry the conductor was? There were only two clarinets in the orchestra. Now he had only one. When my friend went to class the following day, the conductor yelled at him: "Did you understand me when I told you about the concert?" My friend said, "Yes." The conductor said: "Were you absent on purpose then?" My friend said, "Yes." The conductor was furious and said. "Get out of my class." My friend took out his clarinet and played.

                         (*Pei and Fang burst into laughter. At this point Mei*

pops in calling Fang Ying's name.)

Mei: Fang Ying. (*She sees the people in the room and apologizes for her dash.*) Oh. Sorry. I didn't know you are all here...(*Mei greets Pei and Li. The latter return her greeting.*)

Fang: Oh. Mei Lan. This is Nan Shan. I just met him today. (*to Nan Shan*) This is Liang Mei Lan, you must have heard of her, China's famous movie star and pop singer. (*to Mei*) Nan Shan is from Beijing too.

Mei: (*To Nan*) Hi, how are you?

Nan: How are you Miss Liang. I am a staunch fan of yours. I used to follow you from concert to concert. (*To Fang Ying and Pei Hua*) Everyone in China knows Miss Liang Mei Lan, gold record singer and movie star, one of the few being awarded the title of "Artist of the People." It is my good fortune and honor to have the chance to meet you here.

Mei: (*pleased*) Thank you. I'm pleased to meet you too. (*Nan bows to Mei.*)

Fang: (*Noticed Mei's new haircut*) You cut your hair?

Mei: (*Strokes her hair with her fingers.*) Doesn't it look hideous? And I have to go to a wedding this afternoon. And tomorrow I am going to be in New York. They asked me to play Lady Yu in "The King of Chu Biding Farewell to Lady Yu" on Broadway. You know Chen Kai-ke made an award winning film called *Farewell to my Concubine* based on this story?

Pei: (*Exclaims*) Another one going on Broadway!

Mei: Who else is on Broadway?

Fang: Li Yong.

Mei: (*looks at Li, not convinced*) Oh!... Which show?

Li: Don't listen to Fang Ying. I am not going on Broadway. I am trying to break into Broadway.

Mei: (*Her mind is set at ease.*) Oh--!

Li: (*Asks about Mei's Broadway show.*) The Beijing opera or a different version?

Mei: No. They have made it into a Broadway musical.

Pei: Have they? I didn't know that. How did you get the part? Do you have an agent?

Mei: (*superciliously*) No, I don't have an agent and I don't need one. They heard about me. The producer, I mean. And they invited me to talk it over.

Pei: (*Disregards Mai's remark, casually*) Who cut the hair for you?

Mei: I spent $75 for it.

Pei: (*Picks on Mei*) Last week you said you had no money and now you spent $75 for a haircut?

Mei: (*not offended, to Pei Hua*) Last week I had absolutely no money and my refrigerator was completely empty. (*Turns to Fang Ying*) I only had two potatoes and some rotten peas. I was baking the potatoes and boiling the peas when Pei Hua called. Because we talked for too long the potatoes were completely charred. And the peas already rotted but I didn't know. I took a mouthful, errr... (*She makes a disgusted face. Everyone laughs.*)

Li: (*not being sarcastic*) How could China's super star suffer like that?

Fang: She was exaggerating. She always does it for dramatic effect.

Pei: (*to Mei*) I thought you had brought a lot of money with you when you came? You said you were the only one from the Mainland who did not have to work.

Mei: That's true. But I put my money in a 12 month CD account which I cannot touch without being penalized. (*Everyone laughs again*) So I borrowed some money. Those singing engagements are pathetic. The miserable pay is far less than what I was paid in China.

Pei: You are not a superstar here.

Mei: Tell me about it. In China I only gave concerts in huge halls to thousands of eager audiences. Over here, I sing in Chinese restaurants, street fairs, office parties. (*Optimistically*) But this is only temporary. When my Broadway show opens everything will be different. Fang Ying, is Dr. Jones here? I want to find out about my recording contract he is helping me with. I also want to ask for his advice. I am deciding whether to stay on Broadway doing musical or do Metropolitan Opera after I graduate.

Pei: (*in a mocking tone*) Broadway musical and Metropolitan opera, What a rare talent!

Nan: Are you in school, Miss Liang? What do you study?

Mei: (*Vaunts*) American pop music. I will take opera too. My voice teacher said I was best suited for country music though.

Pei: Pop, opera and country. You sure cover a lot of grounds.

Nan: Miss Liang does not need any more training. She is at the top already.

Li: (*casually*) Miss Liang is certainly a big star in China.

Mei: (*Continues to vaunt.*) The Chinese praise me for having a golden voice. To my fans, everything about me it good. (*Changes subject*) Hei, Fang Ying, about my last trip to New York...

Fang: Oh, yes. Have you talked to the Plum Blossom Dance Group.

Mei: I have. I told Li Ching. She's the artistic director, you know. We knew each other for many years back in Beijing. I said "Fang Ying is helping the International Foundation to organize a show. She needs your group to perform in Boston. And she wants to audition you first." She said: "Audition? Why does she want to audition us? Doesn't she have confidence in us? How much is she paying us for the audition? Is she paying for our plan tickets, hotel rooms and meals? Is she compensating us for our lost of work time?" I said "no." And she was all upset. She said "What? she is not paying for these and she wants us to go to Boston for an audition? Who does she think she is? Chairman Mao?"

Li: (*Shakes his head. Makes a casual remark.*) This attitude is not good.

Fang: (*Almost speaks over Li.*) Oh, God, Mei Lan. That was exactly what I predicted they would say. I told you not to ask them for a tryout. Just ask them to come and perform. We will pay them the proper performance fee. 'cause we don't have the budget to pay for all the expenses just to have an audition. But you were so adamant about bringing them up here for a tryout. You said "If you don't they will think you are slapdash and won't respect you."

Mei: (*Makes excuse*) We always have to have tryouts in China. So don't blame me for suggesting it.

Pei: (*Speaks for Fang*) Then, you should have told them that was your idea, not Fang Ying's, so that they would not be mad at her.

Mei: Oh, so you want them to be mad at me, huh? What does it matter if they are mad at Fang Ying. They don't know each other anyway.

Nan: (*Tries to consoles Fang.*) Never mind them. Those show biz people! Always so uppity and difficult. They should be happy to be asked to perform here. I bet they don't have that many opportunities. They think they are still in China?

Mei: (*A little annoyed by Nan Shan's comment*) In China? Huh, there were always a huge crowd of fans following us wherever we went. I always had to sneak out from the back door just to avoid the fans. It's not that we are uppity. We are just so used to the public putting us on the pedestal.

Li: (*Changes the subject*) I got to go. I'd like to work on my script a little today so I will enjoy myself more at Fang Ying's party. Would you excuse me? (*Li gets up to leave.*) Bye everyone.

Fang: You really have to go now.

Li: Yea.

Fang: Then, we'll see you.

Nan, Pei: Bye, Li Yong.

(*Li exits.*)

Mei: Fang Ying, I have a great plan to tell Dr. Jones. I am sure he will be excited to hear it.

Fang: He went to a meeting. You should have made an appointment if you needed to see him. What is you plan?

Mei: Oh, appointment! Why should there be so much trouble? We are collaborators. Why should I need an appointment?

Pei: Appointments save time. They are necessary.

Fang: Mei Lan, Dr. Jones is a very busy man. Everyone has to make an appointment to see him.

Nan: We didn't have that habit in China. We just dropped in at a whim. If people were not there they were not there.

Mei: That's right. Who needs this trouble? (*a change of tone*) This is my plan:

I will form a dance company with all Chinese dancers. I will teach them different kinds of dances from all over the world. Then I will take them on a world tour.

Pei: (*not believing*) You can teach them different dances from …

Mei: (*Cuts short Pei's question*) Of course I …

Nan: (*Speaks over Mei.*) Miss Liang is famous for her dance repertoire from different nationalities. The audience could not get enough of her performance.

Mei: Yea, it's my specialty. Other institutions have asked me to develop this project for them. But I think this is a perfect one for the International Foundation. So I will offer it to Dr. Jones first.

Fang: (*Really means it*) That's nice of you.

Pei: (*to Fang*) I think it is Mei Lan's job to come up with good feasible cultural exchange plans for the International Foundation. (*to Mei*) Isn't that what your H1 status is all about? You are working for the International Foundation, not "Other institutions."

Nan: Oh, Miss Liang works here too?

Mei: (*to Nan. Stretches the truth a little bid*) Dr. Jones asked me to be his advisor on cultural exchange with China. (*Fang takes a look at Mei, understandingly smiled without saying a word.*)

Nan: You are the perfect person for that job. With your clout, you can get things done easily. (*to Fang*) In China contact means everything. Without it, don't even dream of getting things done. Miss Liang can open all the doors in China.

Mei: (*Pleased by Nan's remark*) Nan Shan, you know my reputation and ability. (*Glances at Fang and Pei*) They think I am bull shitting.

Fang: No, no, nobody thinks that.

Pei: We all admire you as a big star in China and everything. But international touring of dance requires extraordinary artistic excellence. Where do you find that many qualified Chinese dancers? If you are to use the beginners that would take forever to train.

Fang: Then there are also all sorts of costs associated with the tour. I'm not sure that the Foundation can raise that much money.

Mei: Ai, the tour will make money for the Foundation. It's not like we are going to perform for free. Let me assure you. This is a money making venture.

Fang: I am afraid it won't break even, much less making money.

Pei: I don't think it will be easy either. If it were reasonably easy why wouldn't others think of it?

Fang: Such as The Plum Blossom group.

Mei: Plum Blossom? They don't have the ability. You don't seem to understand. (*Vaunts again*) Only I can make it happen. I can get dancers from China. The Ministry of Culture will help me. I am good friend with the Minister. I can have the costumes made in China too. Very cheap. The dancers in Beijing are all excellent. You have to see them perform. They are superb. Let me tell you. They are better than the Broadway shows. It won't take long to train them. We can start the grand tour in no time. (*Fang only smiles not being convinced by Mei Lan. Mei realizes that Fang has not taken her seriously. She is a little displeased.*) You don't believe me? You are worried about the traveling expenses? Hotels? Meals? Those are easy. We can ask the airlines to provide free tickets, the hotels to give us free rooms and meals. You just have to write them.

Fang: (*casually*) Do you know how difficult it is to solicit contributions. It's not that simple.

Pei: Unless you have financial backing, this project is not feasible. You will be risking a big financial loss.

Mei: You know what? You people from Taiwan are timid. You are not willing to take risks. Your lives have been too smooth, too easy. You never need to struggle. And you don't like challenges.

Pei: That's not true.

Mei: You don't know a good venture when you see one. (*Sighs*) It's too senseless for me to sing in the Chinese restaurants and dance at outdoor fairs. It's a waste of my talent. In fact it's humiliating. All the people in China would laugh their teeth off if they had heard that I performed dance on the street and changed in the elevator. (*She looks at her watch.*) When is Dr. Jones coming back? There is something else I have to talk to him about. The lawyer said that you had to publicize my position and interview all the applicants. If any one of them has the same qualification as I do, the Immigration Service will deny my green card application.

Pei: That's right.

Nan: The International Foundation is sponsoring your green card? That is great. Miss Liang. You don't need to worry about competition. No one will have your qualifications.

Mei: Nan Shan. Don't tell other people about this, O.K. They will be so jealous.

Nan: Don't worry. Miss Liang, I won't say a word. I don't talk about these things with the Chinese here because my situation is different from theirs. They may be very jealous of me too.

Mei: What is your situation?

Nan: I came with a green card.

Mei: (*surprised*) Oh! that's not bad at all. How did you get your green card?

Fang: Her cousin sponsored him.

Mei: (*skepticlly*) I didn't know that a cousin could sponsor a cousin.

Pei: That is very rare.

Nan: This cousin of mine. She's got money. She owns many businesses--- trading companies, hotels, restaurants, you name it.

Mei: (*Dawned on her*) Oh--! She bought you a green card!

Nan: Something like that.

Pei: That's illegal. I don't think....

Fang: (*Cuts in*) Will the Immigration Service find out? How did she do it?

Nan: (*evasively*) I don't know. She didn't explain it to me.

Mei: As long as you have it and the immigration Service or the court is not chasing after you, you are save. You have nothing to worry. (*changes the subject*) I got to get the green card now!!

Pei: Why is it so important to have it now? Fang Ying and I don't have it.

Mei: You can't do anything here without it. You don't understand. You are in school, studying law. You have tons of money and you don't need to work to support yourself. Without a green card we are not allow to hold jobs.

Nan: How can you work, Fang Ying, if you don't have a green card?

Fang: I am a full time student. working part time is o.k..

Nan: (*Nods.*) I see. Dr. Jones will sponsor you too, I suppose.

Fang: I don't know. I guess I'll finish school first and worry about that later.

Nan: (*to Mei Lan*) How much longer do you have to wait for your green card?

Mei: Who knows.

Pei: Mei Lan, you've been here for only a few months. Normally, you will have to finish school, get a good job. If the employer finds you indispensable he'll apply to the Immigration Service for an H1, after two or three years he will sponsor you for a Permanent Resident status. Then, you'll have to wait for another year or so for approval. The whole process will take many years. You have skipped all the steps. In a year, I think, you will have your green card.

Mei: (*Waves her arm.*) I need to get it sooner!!

Pei: Why in such a hurry? If Dr. Jones had not agreed to sponsor you, what would you have done?

Mei: (*jokingly*) I would have married Professor Steward . (*Turns her head to the side, dramatically*) No. Not that dirty old man. I'd rather be deported than marrying him. (*Turns to Nan*) Let me tell you. That old fool. He showed me his pay slip and said he made $65,000 a year, had a nice condo and a good car. He was trying to buy me with that. That's all I'm worth?

Nan: (*Jokes with Mei*) A professor is not bad. May be he's a little older. So what?

Mei: You have to see him. He gazes at you with one eye but it's that other eye that sees you. His right leg is shorter than the left one. So he walks like this. (*She mimics Prof. Steward's limping.*) He spits all over the place when he talks. And he laughs so loudly, like this (*She mimics Prof. Steward's laugh.*) Good Lord!!!

Fang: I love how Mei Lan mimics people. It's so funny.

Nan: *(flatteringly)* If Miss Liang Mei Lan declares that she is ready to get married, God knows how many guys would wait in line for her to choose.

Pei: *(State the fact.)* I don't doubt that. She already has many suitors.

Mei: But tell me. Which one should I marry? Is there a suitable one?

Nan: Of course one has to have very high qualifications. One has to be young, handsome, rich...

Pei: Mei Lan has several of those. Don't you Mei Lan?

Mei: But there has to have electricity, sparks, I mean. There is not a single one that can kindle any sparks in me. How can I marry any of them? I failed one marriage already. I can't fail again. I'd rather be single for the rest of my life.

Nan: Miss Liang is very open about her divorce.

Mei: How can I conceal it? The whole China knew about it. Didn't you?

Nan: Yes. It was in all the newspapers.

Mei: And it was on the front pages. But no one really knew how and why it happened.

Fang: Do you care to tell us?

Mei: Ai, no need to talk about it anymore. It's none of our fault. The system caused it. He was my first love. We grew up together. We were so young and so much in love. We got married when I was 21. Then we were separated by our jobs. Only a few days a year, around the Spring Festival, did we get to see each other.

Nan: *(Explains to Pei and Fang.)* Many couples lived apart from each other because of jobs.

Pei: Why don't they find jobs in the same city?

Nan: It's not up to us to find jobs. The government assigned us the jobs. During the Cultural Revolution, we were sent to the countryside for thought reform through labor. Husbands and wives were often sent to different parts of China. I was sent to a village outside of Beijing. I was very happy because it was close to my home. But little did I know, I was to work in a brick factory baking bricks. The temperature there was always over120 degree. Can you imagine working 12 or 14 hours a day there? We were all baked dry. And I was not allow to visit my parents.

Mei: How long were you there?

Nan: Sixteen months.

Mei: Only sixteen months? That's not too bad. Some people were sent to the northern or western frontier in the 60's and are still there now.

Nan: I would still be baking bricks there if I had not escaped.

Fang: You escaped?

Nan: Yea. I was in the run and hid for a number of year.

Fang: They didn't catch you?

Nan: China is a big place with over a billion of people. They couldn't find me. And it wasn't that important to find me. After a couple of years I went back to Beijing and the incident was all but blown away.

Fang: Mei Lan, were you sent to the countryside?

Mei: Naturally, that was part of our lives. Nan Shan, because you escaped and was in the hiding you did not experience enough. I went through a lot more than you did although I did not bake bricks. I built road--breaking rocks and carrying the rocks, pushed night-soil-cart, till the land, carrying water and hay. You should have seen me. I was small and thin. The hay stacks were taller than I was. I carried one on my back and bent over like this. (*She bents forward sharply.*) Looking from a distance you wouldn't see me at all. You would only see a big pile of hey moving slowly toward you.

Fang: (*Laughs.*) I like how Mei Lan reenacts her stories. It's so vivid. Every time when I watch her do that and listen to her stories I always laugh tell my stomach aches.

Nan: She's famous for her acting.

Mei: When I went to get the water-- that was one of my daily chores-- I carried two buckets with a shoulder pole. The water was so heavy, I bounced like this all the way. (*She mimics herself bouncing away carrying two buckets of water on her shoulder pole.*) When I got back half of the water was spilled. So I had to walk two miles to get more.

Pei: (*to Nan and Fang*) Mei Lan can do an one-person show, a standup comedy. I guarantee that the audience will laugh. She can derive plenty of funny materials from her experiences during the Cultural Revolution.

Mei: The Cultural Revolution is not funny. (*Fang chuckles at her pun.*) Oh, I have to get going. I still haven't got a gift to bring to the wedding this afternoon. (*to Fang and Pei*) You two, give me some suggestions. what should I get?

Fang: What does your friend want? Usually people give kitchen utensils, small appliances, sheets and towels and so on.

Pei: Yea, those will be fine. Or decorative items.

Mei: Can I just get them President Reagan's picture? (*She laughs.*) Ha-ha.

Fang: (*puzzled.*) What?

Pei: (*similarly puzzled*) Why a picture of the President?

Mei: Yea, President Reagan's picture. My wedding gifts were all Chairman Mao's portraits.

Pei: (*Laughs*) Ha-ha...

Nan: (*Adds a footnote to Mei's statement.*) That was the most common and safe thing to give.

Mei: Big ones, small one, framed ones, posters, pictures fired on porcelain plates and cups, statuaries, buttons. We had all these portraits and no place to put them because the room was so small and we only had one little table and two chairs beside the bed. We filled the table first, then the chairs and the bed. The buttons were pinned on the piece of cloth over the window we called curtain, and on our shirts. At night we reverently remove Chairman Mao from our bed. Before we went to sleep we would report our activities to those portraits, and the first thing in the morning we would ask for instructions from Chairman Mao's portraits.

Fang: You were like a religious fanatic.

Nan: Chairman Mao was no less the God to the Chinese populace than Jesus was to the Christians.

Mei: Even more so. Till this day, I still have my Little Red Book of Chairman Mao's Quotations. I didn't dare to leave it behind when I left China. You know. That total mental control is difficult to be liberated from.

Pei: Hey, why not just give the Little Red Book to your friend as her wedding gift. (*They all laugh.*)

Mei: She'll hate me for life. I really have to go now. (*to Fang Ying*) Set up an appointment with Dr. Jones for me, o.k. Fang Ying? I'll see you all. Nan Shan, it's a pleasure meeting you.

Nan: Hope to see you again soon. Miss Liang.

Fang and Pei: Bye.

(*Mei exits from stage left.*)

Nan: Miss Deng and Miss Ho....

Fang: Call us by our names. Everybody does.

Nan: Thank you, Fang Ying and Pei Hua. I am very happy that I have dropped in here to day. I think you are very nice people. I wish to be a friend of yours.

Lights out

ACT TWO   scene one

>Scene: Same as Act one, a year later
>*Nan Shan sits across the desk from Fang Ying, lights come on.*

Fang: Nan Shan, you really have to study English harder. I cannot be your interpreter forever.

Nan: Just this once, please. This is too important. You have to help me. This medicine is really effective. It will be a shame not to bring it to the American patients.

Fang: If it were really effective whoever invented it would have gotten a Nobel Prize already, and the doctors in the whole world would have been prescribing it. How could the medical world be ignorant of it?

Nan: Everything has a starting point. Right? This is a new cure. The medical world has not heard about it yet. They have to learn about it sometime, somewhere and from someone, Right? That time is now and that some one is me.

Feng: Who told you about this medicine?

Nan: My friends wrote me about it. They said many cancer patients were cured. We can save lives by bringing the medicine to America.

Fang: And you and your friends will make tons of money.

Nan: Very deservedly so. And you too. Fang Ying. You don't think I will forget you.

Fang: Nan Shan you should know it by now. It's not that simple. We all should have ambitions and goals but wild dreams are something else.

Nan: Mine are not wild dreams. (*stand up and walks a few steps to down stage*) They are all very real. But making it in America is not as easy as I have thought. I admit that. It's been 18 months now since I came here. My great plans have all but fallen through.

Fang: (*Gets up and crosses to Nan.*) Because your great plans were all unrealistic. Just be more realistic, Nan Shan. Learn the language. When you try to sell your ideas to the big businesses you can convince them with your eloquent speeches just as you always do in Chinese.

Nan: I agree. You are right. (*a moment of silence*) Fang Ying. You have been a good friend. Good friends should be honest with each other. (*Pauses.*) But I have not been honest with you.

Fang: (*Surprised.*) About what?

Nan: I wanted to tell you this for a long time. I can't conceal the truth about me any more.

Fang: (*curiously*) What is it?

Nan: You know, my cousin who brought me here?

Feng: Yes, the rich cousin who bought you a green card, so to speak.

Nan: No, she is not my cousin and she did not buy me a green card. She bought me!

Feng: (*perplexed*) Huh?

Nan: She bought me. She is a woman from Taiwan originally. She was married to an American businessman, lived in America for 20 years. Her husband died leaving her a good amount of money and his businesses. That year she took a trip to China. We met in Beijing. There was something about me, might be my youth, my looks, my manner, I don't know, anyway, that attracted her. She knew how desperately I wanted to come to America. And said she would do her best to help me. She went back and forth to China a few times that year trying to get me out. Nothing worked. Finally she said the only way was to marry me.

Fang: Oh!

Nan: I was desperately wanting to leave China, and would do anything to make that possible. Marrying her was the only way. And it was not the worst. In fact I was happy. I was willing to give myself to her totally and be loyal and faithful to her for life. When all the necessary procedures were completed I came to America, the land of opportunities, the land of my dream.

Fang: Then?

Nan: I lived in that big house with her, her mother and her son who was in high school. The son hated me and the mother called me a gold digger. I told her that I couldn't take that. She was very understanding. She rented an apartment for me and provided for me. She bought me a new car, new clothes and gave me spending money. That was the time when I first came to this building and met you. You see, all this time I live like a dandy without having to work. Have you wandered how I managed?

Fang: It didn't cross my mind. What happens now?

Nan: I'm not happy with my life. It's funny. I thought I would be loyal and faithful to her forever because she rescued me. But I can't now. I cannot be kept like a pet. My purpose of coming to America is not just to escape China but more importantly to realize my dreams. I told her that I wanted to be free. She agreed to let me go. But, she said my green card was not finalized yet. As soon as I get the card her lawyer will prepare the divorce papers.

Fang: I thought you had your green card from the beginning?

Nan: No. That was another lie I told. But because I am married to an American citizen, I am allowed to hold a job. I can legally stay and not having to go to school.

Fang: That woman is very kind to you.

Nan: I have no question about that. She is a very nice person. But there are so many things that I want to do.

Fang: With her help you can perhaps do those things more easily.

Nan: You don't understand. I feel like a concubine, being owned by her. I need to be free. That's important. All my life in China I did not have freedom. What I want now is a partner to work with me as an equal. She... I always feel that I owe her so much and I can never be her equal. She is a giant shadow towering over me. (*suddenly revealing his inner intention*) Fang Ying, I need someone like you, young, bright, and capable.

Fang: (*Unexpected, unwilling to accept Nan's hint*) Nan Shan, we are friends. That's the best.

(*Pei enters from stage left. She is wearing a business suit.*)

Fang: (*to Pei*) How did it go?

Pei: (*to Nan*) Hi, Nan Shan. (*Answers Fang Ying's question.*) I think they are going to hire me. This is my third interview with them. I'd much rather stay in Boston. So I'm going to turn down the offer in Washington.

Fang: I'm glad. Pei Hua. I'd hate to see you go.

Nan: Congratulations, Pei Hua. Now you are a full-fledged attorney at law. And we can come to you when we need legal advice.

Pei: Certainly. (*to Fang*) Do you still need me to help you with addressing the announcements? I'm sorry that I couldn't do it this morning.

Fang: Don't worry about it. Ding Peng helped me with it and he took them all to the post office.

Nan: I was sorry to be totally useless.

Pei: You see. You should have learned English. This is Fang Ying's first one person show and none of us did anything to help her.

Fang: Don't worry about it. There are plenty of things you can help with. For instance the reception.

Pei: Oh, I'll definitely do that. In fact, I will contribute the whole reception. How's that?

Fang: No, thank you. International Foundation is paying for that. You just be the hostess.

Pei: Are all your work completed?

Fang: Mostly. There is one large piece. Actually it's a set of eight pieces joined together. I am still working on that. The others are at the frame shop. Nan Shan took them there for me. (*to Nan*) Are you sure they will fit in your car when they are framed?

Nan: If they don't I'll borrow a van. (*to Pei*) You know something? When I brought Fang Ying's paintings to the frame shop the guy took a look at the work and said: "This is Fang Ying's work. We framed some pieces for her last year."

Pei: (*curiously*) You could converse with them?

Nan: I had someone with me as a translator. My friend ask the guy how he remembered Fang Ying's style since Fang Ying is not a known artist yet. He said last year shortly after they framed Fang Ying's work there was an art review in the Boston Globe of a group show. One of Fang Ying's pieces was reproduced in the paper. The review praised Fang Ying's art but said that the frame was no good. That's why he remembered Fang Ying (*Pei and Fang both laugh.*)

Fang: If everyone can remember my style like that I will become famous soon.

(*Mei enters with a gift wrapped bottle of wine. The usual greetings among all are carried out.*)

Mei: (*Hands the gift to Fang Ying*) This is for you, Fang Ying. To celebrate your solo art show.

Fang: (*Takes over the gift.*) Thanks. (*Put the gift on the desk while speaking*) Pei Hua is very likely to stay in Boston. She may be joining the firm that she liked most.

Mei: Oh. That's good news.

Pei: It's still too soon to say that. I have to hear from them to say for sure.

Mei: Hm. Everyone has good news. How about you, Nan Shan?

Nan: I don't have good news yet. Still working on it.

Mei: (*In a low spirit*) I'm really tired of everything. My future is a total darkness. My record contract fell through. The Broadway show was a pipe-dream, I am still dragging in school. School is so hard. Half the time I don't understand what the teachers say. I tape the lectures but no one wants to help me anymore. They avoid me when I ask them to translate the tape. Oh Fang Ying. I'm so depressed. What do I do? How long do I have to wait for the green card? Without the green card my plans cannot be carried out. (*sighs*) Sometimes I feel I am in a dead end.

Fang: (*Tries to console Mei Lan.*) You will get your green card soon. Mei Lan. Things will look up for you. I know they will.

Pei: What happened to "The King of Chu Bidding Farewell to Lady Yu?" We never heard you mention it anymore.

Nan: That Broadway production?

Mei: (*At this moment of her low spirit she tells the truth*) Don't even mention it to me. It was never going to be a Broadway production. It was a few Chinese who wanted to make money out of me. Ah, Li Ching's husband was the one who thought about the idea. You know Li Ching, the leader of the Plum Blossom Dance group. They thought with me as the star plus their own dancers they could put a show on stage and make money. What Broadway? They were going to do it in a high school auditorium and pay me $50 a show. Besides, I have to use my old costume that I brought from China.

Pei: You did not accept their terms, I hope.

Mei: We didn't even get that far. They had no singer for the King's role. There were some very good male singers in New York but Li Ching didn't want to pay them. She wanted her husband to play it. Her husband was a flutist in China. He was never a singer, nor a dancer, much less an actor.

Fang: You didn't know the situation at all in the beginning.

Mei: (*embarrassed*) I...

Nan: Those dupers. They are so good at bilking people with fantastic stories. There are many cheaters like that. Mei Lan must not have known the truth before.

Mei: That's right. I didn't know.

Pei: Next time don't deal with these street peddlers. Better do it with a legitimate Broadway producer.

Fang: We learn from our experiences all the times.

(*The phone rings and Fang answers.*)

Fang: Yes. Oh, hi, Attorney Bradley. What's up? Yes, Um. That's good. Mei Lan is right here. I will give her the good news. All right. Thank you. Bye. (She *hangs up the phone. to Mei*) Congratulations. Your case has been accepted. You will get your green card soon.

Mei: (*Overjoyed, put her right hand on her forehead*) Oh! Thank God. finally. I have reached the end of my rope. I was sure that I wouldn't get it.

Nan: Congratulations, Mei Lan. Let's celebrate.

Fang: (*to Mei*) I told you not to worry. You have a strong case. The way Dr. Jones stressed your importance to our program how could the Immigration Service not grant you Permanent Residence?

Mei: (*assumingly*) Now I can tell Hemmingway Incorporated that they can start paying me the salary they owed me. You see I worked there for four months without pay because of my status. But they agree to pay me retroactively when my immigration status changes. Let me see. They owe me..., how much do they owe me?. $90,000 a year, four months would be.... $30,000. (*overjoyed, excited*) Oh, my God. $30,000 now and $7,500 every month.

Fang: You are rich now. Mei Lan. You are all set.

Pei: You can be your old self now. No more depression.

Mei: Finally!!. I've had enough. Just think what I've gone through this year. I was a maid, a security guard, a doorman--doorwoman, I should say, a babysitter...When I worked for that old lady as a maid, she told me to stay in the kitchen or the servant's quarter, not to come out unless she rang the bell. (*pause*) And she gave me the smallest lobster to eat.

> (*Fang laughs. Li enters. Fang and Pei say hi to him. Nan and Mei pay no attention to him but go on talking*)

Nan: Lobster is expensive. It's kind of her to let the maid eat a lobster at all.

Li: (*lost*) What lobster?

Mei: (*Ignoring Nan, she continues*) When I was a security guard for that big company, they gave me a uniform and a hat. Both were too big for me. I had a club hanging from my belt, a walkie-talkie in my hand. I was to walk around all the time. It was at night. Do you think I can fight the robbers with my club? That job killed my feet. When I went home after work I would be walking like this. (*She mimics herself staggering. Everyone laughs.*)

Pei: When you write your memoir one day. You have all these to write about.

Nan: Yes. It's another side of life.

Li: You are talking about our American experiences? They are tough. But when you look back a lot of them were funny too. The first work I did was delivering takeouts. I couldn't drive, and had no license. But the boss didn't know that. My friends all said: "Just pretend you have done it before. Otherwise you will never get a job." So I took the car and tried to drive it without knowing how. I barely got it to the street and it stalled. Not knowing what to do I left the car in the middle of the road and ran to deliver the food.

Pei: Then what happened?

Li: I got fired, of course. Ironing laundry, painting houses, cleaning bathrooms in hotels...Those were not bad if I had a little bit of training and the bosses didn't yell so hard. (*He remembers some funny things and laughs*) Old Pan always tried to find some easy way to paint the walls. When he made a mass and the foreman yelled he said it was better to have some brush strokes shown, more artistic. He put the roller stick on his stomach and go like this (*He mimics the motion,* *swinging his hips forward and backward repeatedly*) He said that would save his energy. Old Liu said to him: "That's too sexy. Don't let the lady of the house see you do that." (*Everyone laughs. The girls blushed.*)

Li: (*Continues*) Little Zhang had the best job as a live-in help. All he had to do was to walk the dogs, feed the bird and did a little yard work. One day the bird, ---a big parrot, said "f. you" to him again and again. Little Zhang got mad and said "zao ni ma" to the parrot. The bird imitated him. "cao ni ma, cao ni ma." He was amused and kept teaching it more. The owner, who was a professor, heard the bird talking in Chinese and was very proud. One day he invited his Chinese students to dinner. The bird spoke to them "cao ni ma, cao ni ma, ta ma de." The proud owner waited for the guests' praise. Instead the guests were dismayed. They asked where had the bird learn such foul language. The professor suddenly realized that he had been fooled. Angrily, he called out: "Little Zhang, come down here." Little Zhang went down and ask what the professor wanted? The owner said: "Did you swear at my bird?" Little Zhang said: "He swore at me first." (*Everyone laugh.*)

Feng: That is funny!! (*turns to Mei*) Mei Lan, $90,000 is a very high salary.

Pei: Remember Professor Steward wanted to impress you into marrying him with his annual salary of $65,000?

Li: $90,000?

Nan: (*to Li Yong*) Yes. Mei Lan will have an annual salary of $90,000 from an American company.

Mei: (*assumingly*) They are not paying me $90,000 because I am pretty, you know. It's because they realized how valuable I would be to their business in China. They will send me to China to secure several deals. Each one of those will bring them tens of millions in profit.

Li: You are going to China?

Pei: Mei Lan will get her green card any day now.

Li: Ah, congratulations.

Nan: When do you think you will go?

Mei: As soon as my green card is in hand.

Nan: I plan to go too. But It will be a while before I can go.

Fang: May be you can go together. You both have a lot of grandiose plans. Why not work together helping each other.

Li: Everyone wants to come to America. And now everyone is talking about going back to China.

Mei: Going to China is crucial at this point. I can lay a lot of groundwork there. I told Mr. Hemmingway about my international touring project. He was very excited. He has money. You know. Oh, he invited me to his house, a huge mansion by the ocean. It has 20 some rooms, a beautiful garden, very big. His servants live in a separate house. They all wear uniforms. I've seen rich Americans living like that in the movies, like... in "Dynasty." He wants me to pick dancers in China. Get costumes made too. He was so receptive to everything I said.

Pei: Oh, so you have turned that project to your new boss.

Mei: The International Foundation didn't want it.

Pei: The International Foundation couldn't send you to China to pick dancers before you get your green card. Right?

Mei: Anyway, Mr. Hemmingway immediately took my idea. Dr. Jones was never so forthright. He hesitated. To me, I will go where there is a road.

Pei: I guess you have to do what's best for yourself.

Li: (*Interrupts Pei Hua*) Hi, everyone, I have something to tell you. I am leaving Boston soon.

Fang: What? Why?

Li: (*a big smile*) I got the job. M. Butterfly. They gave me the part.

Fang: (*joyfully*) Wow. That's wonderful, Li Yong. That's great news. I am so happy for you.

Nan: That is wonderful. Congratulations! That's great. Mei Lan is getting her green card. Pei Hua is going to get her job at the firm of her choice. Fang Ying is going to open her solo show. That's great. Who can deny that America is a land of opportunities.

Fang: All these good news in one day. I don't know whether I can take it.

Li: They want me in Chicago in six weeks. I'll still be doing "The King and I" at school. I hate to leave the show like this.

Pei: Will they let you go?

Li: The Theatre Department was very nice about it. They wouldn't want me to miss the big break. I will be in the show for part of the run and then the understudy will take over.

Mei: That's fabulous. How did it all happen?

Li: You know I went to this agency over a year ago and they told me to go home and study English and see them in a few years? Well, I recently called them. As soon as the lady picked up the phone I delivered a monologue from M. Butterfly. She asked me to see her. I did. Then she got me an audition in Chicago. I got the part.

Fang: As simple as that! My God. Li Yong. You did it.

Li: Yes. But not without a hell of a lot of hard work.

Fang: How did you improve your English so fast?

Li: I did it the only way I knew: The hard way. I tried to learn from TV, radio and movies. I always listen to the dialogues very carefully. And I practiced my pronunciations and intonations by taping my own speech and listening to it. Even when I was in bed I would practice my pronunciations and memorize vocabularies. And I prepared the monologue by doing it every day to the kids that I baby-sat for. The little kids corrected my pronunciations too. The five year old said to me: "Li Yong, it's 'father,' not 'farder.'"

Fang: Gosh, Li Yong. I really admire you.

Nan: Fang Ying, I will treat today, to celebrate all your successes. How about dinner first and go somewhere to dance.

Li: I should treat. But we need another guy.

Mei: I'll treat, of course. Don't even think of taking it away from me today.

Fang: She's making more money now than most people that we know. Let her treat. But if we go dancing we should round up more people. Mei Lan you should call them.

Mei: You call them. I don't want to make it a big fuss.

Feng: Nan Shan and Pei Hua will show off again. How do you guys get to dance so well? (*Returns to the subject of calling people*) Can we each call a few? I hate making so many phone calls.

Li: All right we'll split the list. It's very short noticed. I doubt they will come.

Nan: Call every one. Some of them may be free.

Pei: I got to go home and change.

Lights out

ACT TWO   scene two

> Scene: Same as the previous scene, six weeks later. As the stage lights go on *Li Yong and Pei Hua are on stage.*

Pei: I have thought about it and thought about it. I don't know whether I should tell you this. But if I don't there is no more chance.

Li: There will be. I'll be back. I still have one more semester to go before I graduate.

Pei: I don't think you will come back to graduate. From Chicago you will go on to bigger and better things. A degree is not that important to an actor.

Li: I will be back.

Pei: (*with emotions*) Li Yong, we've been good friends for a long time. I can not hide my feelings any more. I am in love with you. It takes a lot of courage for me to tell you this. I have struggled for a long time. I was hoping to find any sign of mutual feelings in you. But...you don't seem to know...

Li: (*sincerely*) Pei-Hua, I knew all along, you were very nice to me, (*jokingly*) this awkward, clumsy, poor and filthy country bumpkin from Shanghai...

Pei: (*Cuts him short.*) Stop joking.

Li: (*sincerely*) I am very flattered, very grateful, and I really like you too.

Pei: (*disappointed*) Yes. You like me the same way you like all the other guys.

Li: No, Pei-Hua. Not the same way. If I were ready to settle down or have a special relationship, you would be the one.

Pei: You are not ready because you haven't found the right person.

Li: That's not it. You see, I haven't finished my school, I have no money. Now I just got my first professional acting job. There is a long way for me to go.

Pei: That's not a problem. I already graduated from law school and have a good job.

Li: You also have an expensive condo and a new BMW... --and rich parents.

	But those are yours, Pei-Hua. You don't want me to live off of you. I have my pride and my own ambition.
Pei:	I didn't mean that. But I mean, you don't have to worry about supporting me, at least. I will not be a burden to you.
Li:	It won't be fair to you. As an actor, I won't have a stable life. In fact, I expect my life to be....that of a gypsy. That's true. I will get up and go where the job is at a moment of notice. I will not have a home, but to sleep in hotels. That's not a way to have a family. But that is very exciting to me. Theatre is my life, my dream. I can't imagine having a 9 to 5 job, coming home to a house with a white picket fence every day.
Pei:	Li Yong, you don't have to give up your dream. Just let me share your dream. I will be happy just to be part of your life even if it means constant separation. I will visit you wherever you go. We won't have a humdrum life. That's for sure.
Li:	Pei Hua, it really wouldn't be fair to you. I am not ready to make a commitment yet. May be someday...
Pei:	(*sadly*) All right. There is nothing more for me to say. (*She walks away.*)
Li:	(*He walks after Pei.*) Pei Hua, please don't sound so final. Let's still be best friends. I will be very sad if you don't want to be my friend any more.
Pei:	(*a sad smile, tears in her eyes, silence*)
Nan:	(*Pops in from stage left*) Oh, you two are here. Where is Fang Ying?
Li:	She wasn't here when we came.
Nan:	(*to Li*) When are you leaving?
Li:	Tomorrow. I came here to say good bye to Fang Ying.
Nan:	Keep in touch.
Li:	Sure. I will be back too. My good friends are all here.
Nan:	Pei Hua. You are not at work today?
Pei:	No, I took the day off.
Nan:	Today is my day off. It's hell working in the kitchen.
Pei:	(*not in the mood to listen to complaints, she snaps*) Is it worse than firing

bricks? You don't have to escape. You can just quit here.

Nan: (*a little surprised at Pei Hua's harshness, takes a glance at Li, to Pei*) Ah... Something wrong?

Pei: (*impatiently*) Wrong? What could be wrong?

Li: Pei Hua is not in a good mood.

Nan: (*Smiles, as if understanding the situation totally*) Oh... Because Li Yong is leaving. But, he'll be back.

Pei: (*annoyed*) Why don't you shut up. (*in a fit, dashes out of the room from stage left. Nan is embarrassed.*)

Li: Let me go talk to her.

> (*Li runs off from stage left. Nan sits by the desk, grabs a book and begins to read. In a short moment, Fang Ying enters from stage right carrying some files in her hands.*)

Fang: (*not expecting to see Nan here*) You are here! (*put the files on her desk.*)

Nan: Pei Hua and Li Yong were here too when I came. For some reason Pei Hua got upset and left. Li Yong went after her.

Fang: She doesn't like to see Li Yong leave.

Nan: May be she got angry because I said that to her. Everyone can see that she is in love with Li Yong. I don't know why she got angry at my remark.

Fang: Because it hurts her pride. Li Yong is only in love with the theatre.

Nan: (*to himself*) Nothing is easy.

Fang: What did you say?

Nan: Peeling shrimps, wrapping dumplings and wantons, sweeping the floor, cleaning the stove, carrying piles of dishes and huge bags of garbage, be yelled at and threatened by the chef with a big cleaver. That's my daily encounters.

Fang: (*with a little bit of humor*) These are what goes with the territory, a kitchen-help's professional hazard.

Nan: (*Matter-of-factly*) I suppose so. Pei Hua didn't want to hear me mentioning it. She said it wasn't as bad as firing bricks. But I wasn't abused by the other workers in the brick factory. Here, they always swear at me in Cantonese that I don't understand. I just block myself out, not listening to their voices or seeing their faces. I keep thinking about my plans and I said to myself. "Never mind these stupid people. One day I'll show them." (*taking out two newspaper ads and two application forms to show Fang*) Fang Ying, look at these ads. This place wants an automobile mechanic and this one wants an electrician. I think those must be better jobs than kitchen help. So I went and got these application forms. Will you help me filling them out?

Fang: Auto mechanic and electrician? Those are technical jobs.

Nan: But I can fix cars and do any kind of electrical work. I did all sorts of things before. I can do these.

Fang: But they require licenses. Do you have them?

Nan: No, I don't. But I can show them and convince them.

Fang: No way. Nan Shan. You have to have a license in order to get the job. Forget it.

Nan: (*a change of thought*) Fang Ying, I'm going to try importing goods.

Fang: Not medicine, construction materials, woman's apparel or fresh fish, I hope.

Nan: No. Just grocery items.

Fang: Oh!

Nan: Yes, dry mushrooms, dry shrimps. The dry goods are easy.

Fang: Right. At least they will be easier than importing fresh fish and shrimps.

Nan: If they were packed in ice properly. That still could be done.

Fang: But Nan Shan, I felt like a fool helping you sell the idea to that seafood company.

Nan: (*Smiles in embarrassment.*) I am sorry to have put you through that.

Fang: I often wonder why I always let myself be put in awkward situations.

Nan: Because you are so kind to people. Everyone expects you to help and you don't have the heart to say no.

Fang: You made me sound like a saint. What do you need me to help this time?

Nan: The grocery stuff I can handle. (*as if talking to himself*) But my big plan, I need help to carry out my big plan.

Li: (*Enters from stage left.*) Fang Ying.

Fang: (*Turns toward Li.*) Is Pei Hua o.k.?

Li: Oh, yea. She'll get over it.

Fang: (*to Li, very sincerely*) She is very serious about you. She told me that.

Li: Yes, I know. But now my focus is my career in the theatre. Fang Ying, I am leaving tomorrow.

Fang: I see. Li Yong, the best of luck. I know you will make it big. You deserve it. (*Pauses. with a little sadness*) You know how much we'll miss you.

Li: Thank you for everything, Fang Ying. Thank you for being such a dear friend. I'll call you and keep you apprised of all my activities.

Fang: Yes, Li Yong. You must.

Curtain

ACT THREE

Scene: Fang Ying's studio which is also her apartment. There are paintings leaning against the wall, various art supplies, buckets and cans scattered on the floor.

The time is 1988, two years after Li Yong left Boston. Fang Ying is now a full time struggling artist. Mei Lan went back to China after she got her green card. She was there for over a year as a representative of Hemmingway Incorporated to negotiate several business deals and to recruit dancers for her grand international tour. Nan Shan also went to China after his divorce was finalized and his green card in hand. He has tried to lay ground for his magnificent U.S.-China-trade plan. Now they are both back. Fang Ying invites them over to her apartment for a gathering

As the curtain rises: Fang Ying and Pei Hua are on stage.

Fang: Pei Hua, help me straighten out the place a little bit. I haven't got time to do anything. I was painting all night. Now I am going to buy some stuff at the corner market. There isn't anything for them to eat.

Pei: Don't bother, we can order pizza.

Fang: No. Mei Lan hates pizza. Beside, we haven't seen her for a year and half, and Nan Shan for almost that long too.

Pei: All right, but hurry back.

Fang: I will. (*She grabs her bag and exits from stage right. Pei Hua picks up the scrap paper, paint brushes, cans and so forth from the floor and put them back on the table; pushes the big cushions on the floor to their proper place.*)

(Nan *Enters from stage right.)*

Nan: (*happily*) Pei Hua, how are you. It's been almost a year and half.

Pei: (*Smiles.*) Oh, Nan Shan. It's good to have you back.

Nan: Where is Fany Ying?

Pei: She went to get some grocery. How's everything in China?

Nan: China is different now. People are eager to do business, to make money. You know, the government has loosen up its control. Private industries are allowed somewhat. Large businesses are still in the hands of the government leaders though.

Pei: What did you do there during this time?

Nan: I met up with many important contacts. (*Takes out a pile of business cards and shows them to Pei.Hua*) See. I got these cards. Some I met some I didn't. But they all have my card. It's important.

Pei: What do you expect to accomplish?

Nan: Oh, U.S.-China trade. Years ago, we could only hope to sell Chinese goods to America because China couldn't afford to buy from America. Things are changing now. China has the money and interest to buy now. (*smugly*) This is the time for me to play a role. China is not familiar with America. They need someone like me as a bridge. I have a distinct advantage because I have a green card. I can go back and forth. Most other Chinese can't do that.

Pei: I wonder if Mei Lan is thinking the same thing. It'll be fun to listen to her talking about China.

Nan: Of course, Mei Lan has greater advantages. Her relations with the high level cadres are exceptional.

Pei: (*absently*) Yea.

Nan: (*sudden change of subject*) I thought about you a lot while in China, Pei Hua

Pei: Me? Why me?

Nan: Pei Hua, I always think you are very special. I didn't let you know before because I knew you had Li Yong in your heart. But I do think that we belong together. We are more practical people. You are in law and I am in business. If we put our heads together we can accomplish a lot. And we both enjoy dancing and good at it.

Pei: Nan Shan, these are not the reasons for two people to be together.

Nan: I like you a lot. I guess you don't dislike me.

Pei: That's not enough.

Nan: (*presumptuously*) I mean, if you don't mind, I love you. When I was in Beijing I met a girl, a singer, she looked so much like you. I often went to listen to her sing and went out with her a few times.

Pei: So?

Nan: That was because I missed you. She was just filling in for you.

Pei: (*Chuckles.*) I don't know what to say. But Nan Shan, I have no special feelings toward you. And you know that I love Li Yong.

Nan: But loving Li Yong is a lost cause. He only cares about the theatre. That dreamer. He wants to be the biggest star in show biz. That's so impractical.

Pei: (*Defends Li*) You can't say that. Everyone has dreams. Some dreams will become realities because the dreamer rationalizes the dreams and makes them into a set of goals and unflaggingly pursue those goals. Others may be too wild, too far-fetched, too unmanageable, and they remain dreams forever. I think Li Yong's dream is very close to reality.

Nan: But you can't have him. You are still here and God knows where he is.

Pei: For a while I was going to give up on him, forget him. But I can't. So I decided to take what I have, his friendship. We call each other frequently. Of course he does that with Fang Ying too. I fly to San Francisco, LA, New York, wherever he is to see his shows.

Nan: That lucky dog.

(***Mei*** *Enters from stage right wearing a big smile*)

Mei: Hi, everyone.

Nan and Pei: Hi, Mei Lan

Pei: (*Crosses to her to give her a big hug. happily*) How is it? Does China agree with you.

Mei: Just beautifully.

Nan: When did you arrive?

Mei: Only two days ago. Oh, I am still in jetlag. I only talked with Fang Ying once,--- by the way, where is she?--- then I've been sleeping during the day and up all night.

Pei: Fang Ying went to get some stuff. Tell us about your stay in China.

Mei: Ai, too much to tell. Fang Ying is a full time artist now. I wonder how she's doing, money-wise, I mean. Does she sell enough paintings?

Pei: Hard to say. You know how it is. An artist's income is not steady.

Mei: Fang Ying is a smart girl. She'll manage.

> (**Fang** *enters on Mei's line from stage right carrying a brown bag filled with groceries.*)

Fang: What, are you talking about me? (*put the bag on a table.*)

Mei: (*Jumps over to Fang and hugs her.*) Fang Ying, I missed you so much.

Fang: Everyone missed you too. You lazy bone, never sent us a word. (*Moves to the table and pours soda in the cups. to Pei Hua*) Pei Hua you didn't offer them anything to drink. What a lousy hostess! (*No one pays attention to this remark.*)

Mei: (*Responds to Fang's remark about her not keeping in touch.*) I am sorry but I was really busy, and of course, lazy too.

Fang: How's everything?

Mei: (*Vaunts as usual*) China is wonderful to me. After being away for three years, they are still so warm to me. Oh, you should have seen them. People would stop me on the street and say: "Miss Liang, you are back? We knew you would be back. You wouldn't desert us. You were just visiting America, to better your singing and acting. Then you would come back to us." The taxi driver showed me the cassettes he had in his taxi. Everyone of them was mine. He said: "I cannot go a day without listening to your songs. When will you cut new records"

Nan: The people are loyal to you.

Mei: Film producers wanted to make movies about me. Publishers wanted me to write my autobiography. Large companies fought to offer sponsorship of my show, national touring show, you see. And the businesses, they tore up the contracts signed with European and American companies to sign new ones with me. Because they loved me and wanted me to make the money rather than those foreign companies. But little did they know that I was only representing an American company. (*conceitedly*) I was invited to speak at a business conference. All the big shots from every province attended. They regarded me as the highest authority on U.S.-China trade. Everyone was taking notes. They asked all sorts of questions. This was televised nationwide too.

Pei: (*skeptically*) Could you answer all their questions?

Mei: Of course. Remember I worked at Hemmingway before I went to China. I learned all there was to learn about U.S.-China Trade there. These Chinese companies,--government owned, of course, but the managers were very powerful--hundreds of them, begged me to be the middle person to connect them with American companies.

Fang: Are they paying you to do this?

Mei: Oh, much Better than that. I earn commissions. The usual commission is 2%. But I can get as high as 10%. In some cases, it's up to me.

Pei: (*not believing*) How could that be?

Mei: well, you know. On top of the commissions, I can increase the prices. China openly told me that. Oh, you can't imagine how much my profit will be. In principle, Hemmingway should be making these profit because I was only sent to China to make the deals for them.

Nan: But you are not going to turn them over to Hemmingway, are you?

Mei: I am going to leave Hemmingway. I will give them my resignation in a couple of days. Why should I give away hundreds of millions worth of businesses for a meager $90,000 a year? They can send ten people there and still not be able to get the businesses.

Pei: But, legally...

Mei: They can not hold me to it. They may offer profit sharing to keep me though. There are certain advantages of staying with Hemmingway. For example, I don't need to set up my own office and hire staff. That will be a big saving which is important at the beginning.

Fang: The company paid you to work for them in China. I can't see that they have no right to ask you for the result of your work.

Mei: My contract with Hemmingway did not specify details. Besides, China would not have given the business to Hemmingway's representative. They only want to gave them to me.

Fang: Are contracts binding? Can companies tear them up.

Mei: (*Vaunts*) They normally wouldn't. They only did it for me. They were willing to risk legal consequences.

Pei: That's really something.

Mei: China was exceptional to me. The government gave me 100 acre of land in Beijing to build an international arts institute. I will hire the best teachers of music, art, dance and drama from anywhere in the world to teach there. Fang Ying, I will invite you to teach too. And the Ministry of Culture will help me form a first class dance company to tour the world.

Fang: Gosh, Mei Lan, all your dreams are coming true.

Pei: I am curious. Since these will be done with the help of China, why didn't you do them before instead of wasting a few years time in America?

Mei: No. Before I came to America, China loved me as a first rate singer and movie star. That's all. Now they regard me as an accomplished expert and a patriot who is willing to give up the material wealth of America to dedicate herself to China.

Fang: I see!

Pei: (*slightly sarcastic*) Very admirable.

Mei: (*not paying attention to Pei*) Nan Shan, how about you? Fang Ying said you were in China for a long time too.

Nan: I've made some contacts. But of course they can't be compared with yours. Basically, I want to help China buy high tech equipment from America. I am thinking. There are inexhaustible amount of opportunities to grab, and money to be made. A single person can achieve only so much. If we can join forces...

Mei: You should have said you were trying to help America sell high tech equipment to China instead of China buy from America. Because everyone is trying to sell to China. As for my ventures, I am not doing it by myself. I just make the contacts, get the contracts signed. The details are handled by my brother in Beijing. He has other people to help him too. Over here, I will incorporate a company and, perhaps hire my old supervisor at Hemmingway to be my assistant. She is a shrewd business woman.

Pei: Make sure you can trust her.

Mei: (*Understands Pei's insinuation*) Of course I will. She will be loyal if she can make more than she deserves. I won't let her know my China contacts anyway. So what can she do?

Fang: Mr. Hemmingway promised to fund your international dance tour project. In fact he sent you to China to put together the group. What are you going to tell him?

Mei: What's there to tell? I am quitting his company.

Fang: I mean, ethically, you seem to owe him an explanation. He was so nice and helpful to you. If he had not sent you to China you couldn't have had all those opportunities.

Mei: (*presumptuously*) If he hadn't sent me, other companies would have. Someone like me was hard to find. All the big American companies were looking for people to help with their business in China. But there was only one Liang Mei Lan who could get the business deals.

Pei: (*half jokingly*) Except that no American company could get the deals from you.

Mei: (*Somewhat irritated by Pei Hua's remark.*) Well, I did not take advantage of anyone. They are the ones trying to take advantage of me.

Pei: (*Realizes that her words were too harsh.*) I'm sorry, Mei Lan. I didn't mean to sound that way.

Mei: Really, they were trying to take advantage of me. Hemmingway saw it very clearly that my international touring plan would make lots of money. That was why he was so enthusiastic about it. He was not just going to fund me. He was going to invest in me. Our agreement was that we split the profit fifty-fifty. He would pay the expenses including my salary and performance fee. I was to organize and train the group.

Pei: That sounds like a good deal for you.

Fang: Does China give you a better deal?

Mei: China would not take any profit. They considered the project a service that I render to the people because China would gain international reputation from this tour. I don't even need to pay for the costumes. At best I give each dancer a stipend.

Nan: Are you going to train the dancers yourself?

Mei: I don't even need to do that. But they will put me as Artistic Director, just to aggrandize the group's reputation and impress the audience, you know.

Nan: Yes, at least the Chinese audience in every country will be very impressed. Are you going to perform with the company too?

Mei: I will do one dance in the end, with the group as the background.

Pei: Yes, that's what big stars do.

Mei: (*Changes the subject.*) How is Li Yong and the other guys?

Fang: Li Yong is in LA making a movie.

Mei: Has he been back to finish his school?

Fang: He hasn't had the time. Since he left Boston, he has had one contract after another.

Mei: He is doing well then.

Fang: He is also working very hard, always trying to improve his skills.

Mei: How about the other guys?

Fang: Several of them got married.

Mei: My parents kept pushing me to get married again. I couldn't get them off my back.

Fang: Look, us vagabonds are all still single.

Pei: Because you are a bunch of dreamers. You are not willing to settle down. You don't want white picket fences and dogs. As if those will snuff out your ambitions.

Mei: (*Laugh.*) Listen to her. She sounded like a grandmother. Why are you not married either?

Pei: Me? The man I wish to marry doesn't want to marry me. Those asked to marry me I didn't want to be married to. A classic tragedy. I don't have any grandiose ambition or dream. To marry someone I love, rear some kids, have a good job, live a stable, peaceful life. That's what I want.

Fang: Pei Hua always has a clear head on her shoulder.

Mei: (*Grabs the chance to annoy Pei.*) Poor Pei Hua is still waiting for Li Yong.

Pei: Just because I am not married doesn't mean I am waiting for anyone.

Mei: But you are waiting for Li Yong. Don't deny it.

Pei: I am not denying...

Mei: (*Cuts Pei's line short*) You see. You are admitting it. But dear Pei Hua. Look at you. Such a beautiful girl. A capable young lawyer too. Why focus your heart on Li Yong? Is it worth it? Take my words for it. Never marry a guy who does not love you more than you do him. Really, I am giving you this advice for your own good.

Fang: All right. No more such teasing. You two always...

Pei: (*Very irritated, cuts Fang Ying's remark short.*) I don't see why you care so much about me?

Mei: (*Teases.*) Because we are good friends. You don't appreciate my concern?

Fang: Please stop that bickering. Why do you two always pick on each other?

Nan: No matter. They didn't mean it.

Mei: (*Ignores Nan. to Fang*) Ai. Don't be so serious. Just a little joke. (to Pei) Right, Pei Hua. You are not angry, right? (*Pei gives no response. Mei feels a setback, yarns*) Oh, I'm so tired.

Nan: You didn't sleep well last night?

Mei: What sleep? I'm still in jetlag. Besides, China kept calling and faxing me stuff. It's their day time. They didn't care that I should be sleeping.

Nan: Why did they keep calling you?

Mei: Business. They are eagerly waiting for information. (*to Fang Ying and Pei Hua*) And I haven't got a chance to catch up with any sleep yet. But I already consummated a business deal for them yesterday. (*Takes out some papers from her hand bag and hands one to Pei and one to Fang.*) These are two of the purchasing orders I got. See if you can find the items for me. I will give you 3% of my commission. Sorry, Nan Shan, I don't think you will find any lead. But if you can, here is one. (*She hands one to Nan Shan.*)

Pei: (*Looks at the contract and smiles*) Smart, real smart. You have the ordering company's name whited out so that your gofer in America wouldn't be able to contact the Chinese company directly.

Mei: (*matter-of-factly*) One has to protect oneself.

Pei: (*a late response*) And 3% of your commission? (*hands the paper to Mei*) I can't find any place to buy second hand CAT scanners.

Mei: Try it. You haven't even tried. How do you know you can't find it?

Nan: They asked me to find that also before I came back.

Fang: (*Looks at her sheets of paper.*) Second hand buses? automatic control?--What is automatic control?-- Hospital beds? (*She hands the paper back to Mei Lan too and jokingly*) Mei Lan, why not can-openers and skin lotion like you talked about before.

Mei: (*seriously*) They have those now. Seriously. These things are badly needed. Try to get them for me. I don't have time to do it myself. I only have two months here and I am recruiting singers and dancers.

Fang: I thought you were recruiting them from China.

Mei: Oh, no, this is something else. I have signed contracts with all the big cities in China. I am taking American performers to tour China. The idea excited them. They haven't seen any American shows, you know. In a few years, other people will bring similar shows to China and they will lose their novelty and money won't be as easy to make.

Pei: Gosh, Mei Lan, you recognize an opportunity when you see one.

Mei: (*proudly*) This is called having business brain. I will be very busy auditioning performers in the next couple of weeks. And buy stage wardrobe for myself, and may be for the performers too. There are tons of things to do. You can't imagine how complicated it can get. This is a group of 30-some people, plus instrument, costumes. Oh...I already feel dizzy just thinking about it.

Nan: Do you have a manager?

Mei: Yes, thank God. This is a very experienced stage manager. His duties are not limited to managing the show on stage. He will assist me in all aspects of the project. And he is not going to charge me much. Because he was all elated about the opportunity to see those places in China. I will tell the performers that this is their best chance to see China, a hundred times better than if they join a commercial tour. And their trip will be paid for. That should be counted as a big portion of their pays.

Pei: Is your manager a Chinese?

Mei: No. I want him to manage the 30-some young Americans. A Chinese won't do.

Pei: I think you need a Chinese manager to deal with the logistics in China.

Mei: (*Thinks that this is a favor to Pei Hua.*) Do you want to do it, Pei Hua.

Pei: No, not me. I think Nan Shan will be an ideal candidate. (*to Nan*) would you like to do it?

Fang: Yea. I think Nan Shan will do a great job. That is if Mei Lan will hire a Chinese manager and Nan Shan is free to do it.

Nan: I...I think it will be fun. And I can handle it smoothly so that Mei Lan does not have to worry about a thing.

Mei: Let me think about it.

Fang: Will you all come to the kitchen. I need your help to prepare food.

>(*Fang picks up the grocery bag. Everyone follows her to the kitchen.*)

lights out

ACT FOUR

> *Scene: Fang Ying's studio and apartment, a year later, 1989.*
> *As the lights go on Nan Shan is sitting in a chair.*
> *Fang Ying brings a plate of snacks to the coffee table.*

Fang: (*Sits in another chair*) I was very sorry that I couldn't go to your wedding. The opening reception of my solo show was on the same day. If it were in Boston I could have....

Nan: I would prefer to have it in Boston. But Stacy thought it would be nice to have the wedding at her parents' house.

Fang: How did you and Stacy talk to each other. Do you speak enough English now?

Nan: No. But Stacy speaks some Chinese. She studied it in college.

Fang: (*with a little humor*) And her Chinese is getting better all the time because you never try to speak English with her.

Nan: (*a little embarrassed*) You know learning a second language is nearly impossible for me.

Fang: I wonder who will be the next. Our bachelor group will soon be disintegrated.

Nan: How about you, Fang Ying. When will we hear your happy news?

Fang: (*Gets up and walks down stage*) I'm not in a hurry to get married. I think marriage is a very serious matter, a life long commitment. Unless I feel that one special person is an indispensable part of my life, like the way Pei Hua feels about Li Yong, I will not make that commitment. Right now, As Mei Lan said: No one has kindled the sparks in me yet.

Nan: (*Walks to Fang*) Pei Hua used to say that we were dreamers. And dreamers didn't want to be tied down, especially me. I struggled to regain my bachelorhood and soon afterward, I gave it up again.

Fang: (*concerned*) You didn't rush into it, I hope.

Nan: No. Stacy is very nice to me. Even during our first tour in China she openly showed her affection toward me. Mei Lan was not pleased. She said we should have kept a strict professional relation. She didn't say anything to Stacy but she sure did to me. And I had to warn Stacy about it. Mei Lan almost did not want Stacy to go the second time. But she didn't have a dance as good as Stacy so she had to put up with her. --- We were much more discreet this time. After the second tour Stacy quit, --- and I quit.

Fang: Mei Lan did three tours altogether, didn't she? I didn't see her at all between her tours. She said she was too busy to see me.

Nan: Yea. I stayed in China between the first and the second tours.

Fang: Were the tours very successful?

Nan: The first one was good because it was something new. The Chinese people was curious about what American entertainers were like. But they weren't thrilled. The newspapers reports were short and lacked enthusiasm. The audience's response to Mei Lan was lukewarm. During the years when Mei Lan was gone China produced some fine young entertainers. They are pretty and they can sing better. Mei Lan is not the superstar she used to be. It's very sad. But she still made a lot of money though.

Fang: (*referring to Mei's limited success*) Is that why she decided not to do it anymore?

Nan: May be. She also realized, I think, without me it would be impossible for her to deal with all the little crises. They were crises, honestly.

Fang: She could find someone else. Couldn't she?

Nan: (*Smiles.*) Trustworthy and honest people are hard to hind. Even her brother cheated her.

Fang: I'm sure Mei Lan appreciated what you had done.

Nan: I sure hope so. But I don't think so. Mei Lan doesn't appreciate other people's effort. She blames much more than she praises. No one can work with her for long.

Fang: Oh, Nan Shan, I think these tours have done much damage to your friendship.

Nan: No. That's not it. But they gave me the opportunity to see Mei Lan as what she really was. I'm not upset with her. I'm just disappointed. These are my very objective observations of Mei Lan. I thought so highly of her before not only because she was a big star but also because she was a capable woman with a great deal of ambition.

Fang: She is a smart business woman. She was able to achieve a lot while other people failed.

Nan: She also impresses people more than the reality.

Fang: What do you mean?

Nan: All those deals she talked about a year ago, none of them has been consummated. Those contracts that Chinese companies signed with her, they were torn too.

Fang: What? She said China was particularly good to her so they tore old contracts to sign new ones with her.

Nan: Well, they did the same to her.

Fang: How could they do that? Isn't it against law? There must be some kind of law. Is there?

Nan: They did not sign the contract with her because they loved her. It was because they thought she could deliver what they wanted faster. You see, she gave them that impression---when she couldn't fulfill her promises within the contractual period they turned away.

Fang: Oh!.

Nan: She should not have grabbed everything. She made promises to hundreds of businesses and at the same time she spent all her time on the performance tours. If she only took on one or two and concentrated on getting them done on time she would have come out well. This is hindsight, of course, if she were not so greedy and stayed at Hemmingway Incorporated, with their large network, manpower and capital, they would've accomplished something.

Fang: Then business would keep coming in. But remember, you sort of encouraged her to take the business and run.

Nan: (*embarrassed*) Yes, I did.

Fang: (*Smiles and half seriously.*) So, excuse me for saying so. But it's easy to criticize other people.

Nan: (*softly, apologetically*) I know. And I'm sorry.

Fang: What are you doing these days? I mean business-wise.

Nan: Stacy's father has a construction business. I am helping him.

Fang: Construction business? You mean building houses?

Nan: Yea.

Fang: Oh. You told me that you built a house in Beijing by yourself. So this is right in your alley.

Nan: The house in Beijing? That's just a shed. And one time there was a storm. The house was blown to the ground.

Fang: Make sure you build better ones for the clients.

Nan: He won't let me do any construction work. Just painting the walls, tiling the floors and stuff.

Fang: (*with humor*). No more high-sounding plans?

Nan: They are temporarily put to rest. May be permanently put to rest. One has to be practical, especially when one becomes a father.

Fang: (*Eyes open widely.*) Are you going to be a father soon?

Nan: (*Smiles.*) Yes.

Fang: Oh, congratulations.

Nan: Thank you. There are no more dreams. Pei Hua's description of a humdrum life--white picket fence, a dog and a couple of kids. That will be my life.

Fang: That's the American dream. It's not so bad.

                        (Mei *calls from offstage)*
Fan Ying, Fang Ying.

Nan: (Ignores Mei's call.) Why do we struggle so hard to come here though?

                        (*Mei enters on Nan's line. She has two packages of gift in her hand.*)

Mei: (*Sees Nan.*) Ai, you are here early, Nan Shan. (*Hands one gift box to Nan*) Here, a belated wedding present for you and Stacy.

Nan: Oh, thank you. You shouldn't have.

Mei: Don't mention it. (*She hands another gift box to Fang Ying*) This is for you.

Fang: For me? Oh, Mai Lan, you shouldn't have. (*takes over the box.*)

Mei: Open it. Open it!!

Fang: (*Tears the wrapper, opens the box, takes out the gift, surprised, joyously*) A pair of straw sandals! Oh, Mei Lan. Thank you so much. Where did you find them. You said China didn't have these anymore.

Mei: (*very sweet as usual when she wants to*) I must find them for you if I had to search the whole of China. Everywhere I went I looked for them. Finally in a small rural village I found them.

Nan: (*to Fang Ying*) Why do you like straw sandals so much? The peasants don't even wear them anymore. Aren't these too big for you.

Fang: I'm not going to wear them. I just want to have them. (*Holds them high and looks at them admiringly*) Aren't they the most beautiful thing? May be I will hang them on the wall.

Mei: (*Smiles, lovingly*) Artist! I don't know.

Fang: (*Crosses to Mei Lan to hug her*) Thank you. It's good to have you back, Mei Lan. I hope you won't go away anymore.

Mei: (*happily*) I have something to tell you. You will never guess it.

Fang: What is it?

Mei: (*Lifts up her left hand to show her ring*) I am going to get married.

Nan: (surprised) Oh---

Fang: (*happily surprised*) Get married? To whom. You rascal, you! Keep it a secret from me, eh?

Mei: It's a new development. I didn't expect it.

Nan: Who is the lucky one?

Mei: (*playfully*) Guess.

Fang: Zheng Wei? (*Mei shakes her head*)..Huang Kan? (*Mei shakes her head again.*) Who? I can't guess it. Is it some mysterious man you met abroad.

Mei: (*Laughs*) No, It's Louis Hemmingway.

Fang: Louis Hemmingway? The "Hemmingway Incorporated" Hemmingway?

Mei: (*Laughs again*) Yes.

Nan: That's a surprise. We were just talking about him.

Mei: I never mentioned this to you. But he had his eyes on me since I first worked for him. He invited me to his house,-- that mansion by the ocean, took me to operas and plays--I didn't enjoy the plays; I didn't understand them. He told me he was divorcing his wife. (*Explains*) Not on account of me though, you see. They couldn't get along for years. But I didn't want to be involved in that kind of a situation. People would think I was a home-wrecker. I also thought he was too old?

Fang: How old is he?

Mei: He's 53 now.

Fang: That's not too bad. (*banteringly*) You kept in close touch with him even when you were hiding the business deals from him?

Mei: I didn't really take the businesses from him. I haven't got time to do them.

Fang: When did this happen? How did he bring this up, I mean how did he find you and propose to you?

Mei: I bumped into Elisa in a party. You know the woman who used to be my supervisor at Hemmingway's. Well she told me that Louis talked about me and wonder how I was doing. She said I should give him a call. So I did. He was very happy. He invited me to dinner. We talked about my trips.

Fang: But you must have also talked about the business opportunities you had in China.

Mei: In fact I didn't. He told me that he had missed me a lot and ask if I would marry him.

Fang: Were you surprised?

Mei: Yes, I was. But I accepted it. (*with a victorious grin*) This marriage will bring together two rare power-houses. He has money and connections here. I have the best connections in China. No one can compete with us in U.S.-China trade business now.

Nan: Mei Lan is always ahead of everyone. Will you continue with your performance tours?

Fang: Oh, yes, how about your international tour?

> (*Li Yong and Pei Hua enter on Fang's line. Pei Hua has a brown grocery bag in hand.*)

Pei: Sorry we are late. (*Hands the grocery bag to Fang Ying.*) Just some fruit.

Fang: (*Takes over the bag.*) Thanks.

> (*Fang brings it to the kitchen. Everybody greets one another.*)

Li: (*to Mei*) How's your tour in China?

Mei: The performance tours were too tiring. Nan Shan knew how it was. Two or three days at a city. The kids, I mean my performers, some of them got sick. They were not used to the food. They liked Chinese food, the kind they got here. But when they had to eat bean sprouts and tofu every day, they couldn't take it. Toward the end every one lost weight. Their clothes were torn. They looked like beggars.

Pei: (*Laughs with everybody*) Mei Lan. Things sound funny when they are from your mouth.

Fang: Mei Lan has an exceptional news to break to you. Mei Lan, tell them.

Mei: Oh, I am going to get married.

Li and Pei: Oh, that's good news.

Li: We have something to tell you guys too.

Fang: (*expectantly*) What is it?

Pei: Li Yong and I are going to get married too.

Fang, Nan and Mei: (*Surprised, happily*) Really?

Fang: Oh, I am so happy for you.

Mei: This is the most pleasant surprise.

Nan: Li Yong has finally decided to settle down.

Pei: But not in a house with a white picket fence and a dog.

Li: But I realized that dream and reality can co-exist.

Fang: Li Yong, yours is not a dream. It is a clear goal. You have worked hard to achieve it.

Pei: He has an unshakable determination and willpower. He does not let anything affect them.

Li: An actor's road is not a straight and even one. But I don't complain about it. I just try to do my very best. Try to learn as much as I can. In New York many Asian American actors criticized me for being aloof to their cause when I refused to join in their demonstrations and petitions. The way I look at it, if you are really, really good, you will have your break. Complaining won't solve anything.

Pei: You know, Li Yong will play the lead in Miss Saigon on Broadway. And he has two film contracts.

Mei: That's fantastic. Pei Hua, how did you catch him?

Li: Pei Hua is wonderful and loving. I finally realized how lucky I had been for all these years.

Mei: (*not particularly intentional but shoots out her usual caustic remark at Pei Hua*) What are you going to do after the marriage, following Li Yong around?

Pei: (*Displeased, but controls herself*) No, I am not going to follow him around. I will still practice law in Boston. The next two years he will be in New York. We can see each other every week. Even when he is in other cities, I can still visit him.

Fang: Have you told your parents?

Nan: This calls for a big celebration. (*No one pays attention to his remark.*)

Pei: (*Responds to Fang's question*) Yes. I have.

Nan: Two big news in a day. (*Still no one pays attention to his remark.*)

Fang: (*to Pei*) What did they say? Did they object? They didn't want you to enter the theatre field and now you are marrying an actor. It's so ironic.

Pei: Exactly. They tried to stop me, of course. But I'm not listening this time.

Fang: Good for you.

Pei: Yea. My mother used to say: "I don't tell you what you should do or not do in life. You have the brain, so you have the freedom too. There are only three things that I will decide for you. One is your field of study, one is your career, and the other is your marriage. (*Everyone laughs.*)

Li: (*with humor*) That's about it.

Pei: Well, I did listen to them on my field of study and choice of career.

Li: Forgive us, Mei Lan. We have not asked you. Who is the lucky guy.

Mei: Louis Hemmingway of "Hemmingway Incorporated."

Pei: Oh--, old boss. Was this an old secret romance that you didn't tell us about.

Mei: No, no. This is a new development.

Pei: (*Returns a biting remark with a smile*) Now you can be business partners. Your business deals in China will be kept in the family. No profit will leak out.

Mei: (*Getting the point, sensitively*) He has no idea about any deal in China. He asked to marry me because of me.

Li: (*sincerely*) Of course. What other reasons could there be?

Mei: Pei Hua seems to think that Louis is interested in my business deals in China.

Pei: No, I didn't mean that. I mean from now on you won't hide those lucrative business deals from him anymore.

Fang: None of that, Pei-hua. (to Mei) Hemmingway is a very rich man. He would not care for those deals to marry someone. You are beautiful and talented. A lot of people are attracted to you. But only Hemmingway is qualified to ask for your hand.

Mei: (*Pleased by Fang's remark.*) You are good with words.

Li: Are you still going to take Chinese dancers on international tours? I think you should.

Mei: I will. All those things I always wanted to do, I will do them. Just be a wealthy man's wife, go to parties all the time? No. that will bore me to death. Louis said he would support everything that I wanted to do. With his money and our heads together we can monopolize U.S.-China trade for good.

Pei: Did he say that?

Mei: (*proudly*) Yes.

Pei: (*being sharp again*) I thought Hemmingway was not interested in your business deals in China.

Mei: (*irritated*) It was not the reason why he proposed to me.

Pei: But this marriage will definitely give you what you want.

Mei: What's wrong with that? Sure, I can build my international arts institute in Beijing. I can take my performing group on international tours. Do it the grand way. Not like how I did it in China. As you, Pei Hua, have said, "got to have financial backing." Money is the key. Without it you can only have dreams. Now my dreams will come true. (*Turns to Fang Ying. Changes the subject*) Fang Ying. You are the only one left. When will you get married?

Fang: I'm still waiting for that electricity, the sparks. I have not given up my dream to become a great artist.

Curtain

THE END

www.ingramcontent.com/pod-product-compliance
Lightning Source LLC
Chambersburg PA
CBHW051755040426
42446CB00007B/385